LIFTING THE LID

G000294638

Ursula Barry was born in Co. Tipperary, Ireland in 1953. She works as a lecturer and researcher. Over the past twelve years she has become a well-known activist on women's issues, environmental issues and in support of democratic rights. She is the author of a number of papers highlighting the position of women in the Irish economy and has given numerous talks to women's groups and community groups on the economy and the environment. Ursula Barry was the joint editor of *Information Technology – Impact on the Way of Life* (Tycooly International 1982) and the research/editorial co-ordinator for *Who Owns Ireland, Who Owns You* (Attic Press 1985). She is currently lecturing on the Irish Economy and on Urban Sociology in the College of Technology, Bolton Street, while continuing to actively pursue her own research interests.

First published in 1986 by
Attic Press
44 East Essex Street,
Dublin 2

Barry, Ursula
  Lifting the lid: a handbook of facts and information on Ireland.
  1. Ireland — Social conditions
  I. Title
  941.5   HN400.3
  ISBN 0-946211-26-4
  ISBN 0-946211-25-6 Pbk

Cover Design: Catherine McConville
Book Design: Jole Bortoli
Typesetting: Phototype-Set Ltd., Dublin
Printing: Brough, Cox & Dunn, Belfast
Assistant Researcher: Mary O'Connell

The publishers gratefully acknowledge the following for permission to reproduce illustrations and photographs for which they hold the copyright; Robert Armstrong; Jole Bortoli; Fergus Bourke; Bulbul; Jimmy Burns, New Hibernia; Siobhan Condon; CREW; Brian Fitzgerald; Irish Times; ISIS; Tom Mathews; Derek Speirs; Women's Community Press; YEA.

The publishers also wish to thank Siobhan Parkinson, Helen Litton, Maria Walsh and Colette O'Neill and everyone else who helped to make this book a reality.

LIFTING THE LID

HANDBOOK OF FACTS AND INFORMATION ON IRELAND

Ursula Barry

Attic Press, Dublin.

Acknowledgements

I would like to express my real appreciation to Mary O'Connell who put together an enormous amount of material in a very short space of time. Without her willingness and ability to extract reports and publications from hundreds of groups and organisations, this book would not have been possible.

I would like to thank Pauline Jackson for all the encouragement and support over the years and my publishers Mary Paul Keane and Roisin Conroy for their patience and commitment. Finally my special thanks and love to Melissa Murray for reading countless drafts, her helpful suggestions and of course the toasted sandwiches.

Assistant researcher Mary O'Connell would like to thank Eddie Conlon, Derek Dunne of Magill Magazine, Sandy Fitzgerald of the Grapevine Arts Centre, Tim Jackson of the Irish Council for Civil Liberties, Bryan Lucas at the Central Statistics Office, Moirin Moynihan, Margaret Muir, Patricia McCarthy, Melissa Murray, Alan MacSimóin, Deirdre McCartan and Luke Gibbons of the NIHE, Patricia O'Donovan, Equality Office of ICTU, Paula O'Hare at FLAC, Tony O'Toole of ACRA, Monica O'Connell, Sue Richardson, Ruth Riddick, Anne Speed and the Simon Community.

Very special thanks to Ann Maguire, Anne O'Leary and Teresa O'Connor.

Dedication:
*To Cormac
growing up in a Free State
and Emma
who has just arrived here.*

Ireland — Some Basic Facts

Ireland comprises 32 counties. 26 counties are known as the Republic of Ireland, the remaining north-eastern counties, known as Northern Ireland are under British rule.

Total Population (1981 figures)
Republic 3,443,405
Rural population 44%
Urban population 56%
North 1,509,892

Area
Republic 27,136 square miles
Capital: Dublin
North: 5,459 square miles
Capital: Belfast

Age breakdown (Republic).

Years	0-14	15-44	46-64	65+
	30%	42%	17%	11%

Birth Rate (Republic) 20.3 per thousand.

Infant Mortality Rate (Republic) 10.6 per thousand live births.

Religions
Republic 95% Roman Catholic by birth
North   30% Roman Catholic by birth
Republic 5% Protestant by birth
North   65% Protestant by birth

Languages
Republic
First Official   Irish
Second Official English
North   English

Currency
Republic Punt (Irish Pound)
North Sterling (English Pound)

Voting Age Over 18. Those excluded from voting includes prisoners and disabled persons unable to attend a voting centre.

Houses of the Oireachtas (Parliament consist of Dail Eireann (Lower house) 166 members and Seanad Eireann (Upper house) 60 members.

Fianna Fail	72
Fine Gael	69
Labour	14
Progressive Democrats	5
Workers Party	2
Independents	4

Government:
Fine Gael and Labour Coalition.

North: 17 members are returned by Northern Ireland constituencies to the House of Commons, Westminster, England.

Democratic Unionists	3
Official Unionists	10
Social Democratic Labour Party	2
Sinn Fein	1
Ulster Popular Unionist Party	1

Proportion of Women on Executives of Major Political Parties

Fine Gael	13%
Fianna Fail	8%
Labour Party	17%
Workers Party	6%

Proportion of Women	Candidates	Elected
Local Government	12%	8%
Dail/Seanad	14%	9%

Sources: Council for Status of Women 'Who Makes the Decisions? Women on the Boards of State Sponsored Bodies (1985)'.
Ailbhe Smyth *Women and Power in Ireland: Problems, Progress, Practice,* Women's Studies International Forum Vol 8, No 4, 1985.
Jean Tansey, *Women in Ireland,* Council for the Status of Women 1984.
Institute of Public Administration Yearbook and Diary 1986.

REPUBLIC: Number and Proportion of Women in Selected Political Elites		
	Number	Proportion
Ministers	3	10%
Seanad	6	10%
Dail	14	8%
Local Councillors	71	8%
European Parliament	2	13%
Ambassadors	1	3%
Judges	6	7%
Directors of top 20 companies	1	0.1%
Directors of top 4 banks	2	3%
Employer-Labour Conference	0	0%
Union Executives (9 selected Unions)	21	13%
University Deans	5	1%
Executive Positions in Radio Telefis Eireann (RTE)	21	9%
Newspaper Editors (national)	0	0%

Number of Women on Administrative Boards of Selected State Sponsored Bodies		
	Numbers	Number of Women
Aer Lingus	16	1
AnCO (Industrial Training)	14	0
Arts Council	17	6
Bord na Gaeilge (Irish language)	12	3
An Foras Taluntais (Agriculture)	10	3
Health Education Bureau	10	3
Higher Education Authority	19	3
Industrial Development Authority	9	0
Legal Aid Board	13	4
Medical Council	25	4
National Board for Science & Technology	9	1
National Economic and Social Council	23	2
Nuclear Energy Board	7	0
Radio Telefis Eireann (RTE)	9	1

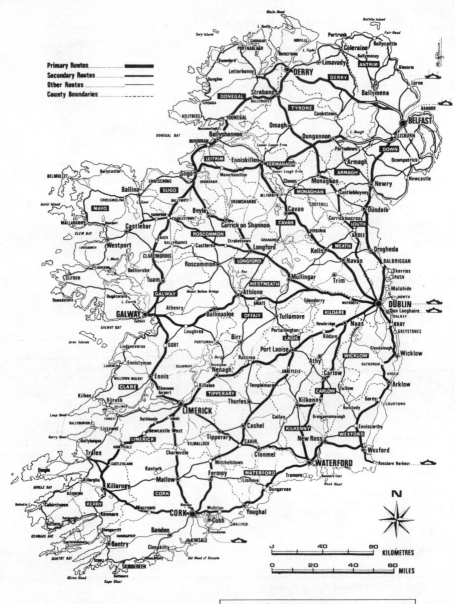

Primary Routes
Secondary Routes
Other Routes
County Boundaries

Belfast — Douglas, Liverpool
Cork — Pembroke, Roscoff
Dublin — Douglas, Holyhead, Liverpool
Larne — Cairnryan, Stranraer
Rosslare — Cherbourg, Fishguard, Le Havre, Pembroke

CONTENTS

Introduction

This book is an attempt to lift the lid off some aspects of our lives on this island, to get below the surface and peer into a few dark corners. *Lifting the Lid* brings into focus the oppression and exploitation generated by a dependent patriarchal capitalist system. In a society that is tiered in accordance with one's economic wealth, women are often pushed to the bottom of each layer. Women have not, as yet, established the economic and social independence necessary to facilitate our self-reliance and freedom. One step towards changing this is developing an awareness of our economic oppression, and ultimately, through a process of self-determination, alongside other forces for change, rejecting *any* system which validates existing oppression.

Lifting the Lid is divided into three sections: Economy in Crisis, Repression and the Law and Social Control. It deals with issues as wide apart as the arts and unemployment, the church and poverty, the environment and family law. It is a reference and information book primarily for women, but also for anyone interested in analysing the society we live in. The reason for writing and publishing *Lifting the Lid* is to inform, but also to expose the misinformation which is being handed out to us on a daily basis. *Lifting the Lid* takes and uses information as *one* source of power in this society. Ireland has no freedom of information act. The right to information is a struggle which must confront bureaucracy and powerful interests backed by political control. Taking control of our own lives involving new ways of thinking, living and working, is a critical part of women's struggle worldwide.

Lifting the Lid draws on scores of reports, books, papers and pamphlets, presenting existing material in a short and hopefully easy-to-read format. Graphics and illustrations are used throughout to make the information as accessible as possible.

Lifting the Lid examines many of the different facets which make up Irish society. In the first section 'Economy in Crisis', the roots and implications of the economic crisis are placed under a microscope. The stripping of our economy through debt repayments and profit exportation as well as the depletion and misuse of our natural resources, aided and abetted by the state, are all highlighted. Statistical information in relation to women and work, agriculture, services and manufacturing industries is used to illustrate the unjust distribution of wealth and work in this country. The exclusion and segregation of women both inside and outside the formal economy is examined to indicate the particular economic exploitation of women.

A close look at state schemes exposes the blatant discrimination implicit within all of these schemes, against women. For one reason or another the majority of women with children are denied participation in such schemes.

How can any government justify a system, particularly a tax system, which benefits the wealthy and causes severe hardship to those in need? Personal and income tax codes are shown for what they are — penalties imposed on the poorer and working classes. A brief look is taken at some of the wealth owners and money spinners who are doing so well even in these times of recession.

Moving into the second section 'Repression and Law', *Lifting the Lid* explores the reality behind our family law legislation and the resulting administrative confusion. The devastating defeat of the recent divorce referendum leaves thousands of women, men and children trapped in this legal morass with little hope of effective change. Right wing groups, backed by the catholic church swung the vote in the face of an inept government campaign, the limits of the Divorce Action Group and the cynical political manoeuvring of Fianna Fail. While legislative change, demanded and fought for by the women's and feminist movement of this country, has been significant over the last decade (including contraception, equal pay and married women's rights), its impact remains weak without a fundamental upheaval in social attitudes and a radical restructuring of our social system.

Paralleling the changes that *have* taken place is the continuous erosion of basic democratic rights in both the six and twenty-six counties. *Lifting the Lid* examines the 'states of emergency' which have institutionalised extensive powers for the security forces on both sides of the border.

The concept of crime, what it is and who are the criminals is questioned and challenged. Criminalisation as a system of control and the realities of women's crime as a result of social deprivation are investigated. *Lifting the Lid* looks to those who have lost their liberty at the hands of the twenty-six counties state, imprisoned in vindictive penal institutions which cannot even guarantee their health and survival.

In the final section 'Social Control' *Lifting the Lid* turns to the widespread deepening poverty both north and south as unemployment marginalises more and more people, never to find a job or earn an income. Humiliation is the key word within the welfare system. Again it is women and other oppressed groups such as travellers and the homeless who take the brunt of this inept and discriminatory structure in which arbitrary decisions by individuals can deny us our rights. A prevailing and active policy of social control permeates every part of our society from the family unit to the educational and health systems. The pattern of control, strongly influenced by the catholic church is directed more and more towards women, denying us access to facilities to control our fertility and express our sexual needs and choices. By delving into the media, the arts, the physical and social environment, *Lifting the Lid* brings together critical aspects of cultural, political and economic life in this country.

No single publication can tell the full story — *Lifting the Lid* does not uncover everything. Facts and statistics are never neutral and they require more analysis than these pages would allow. I hope it can provoke questions, arguments and debate. It is not a book of answers, but rather an attempt to paint a very different picture to the smug and complacent images so often peddled by the media and the state. It is a depressing picture, because *Lifting the Lid* stands opposed to those who glibly speak of cutting public services while refusing to confront the poverty, homelessness, ill-health, derelict housing, cultural domination and oppression of women which characterise this society.

Lifting the Lid provides the basis for change. Information is one form of power, when we have it it allows us to question, understand, organise, change and then take control.

URSULA BARRY, JUNE 1986

Between 1980 and 1985 £4034 million in profits was taken *out* of this country by multinational companies.

●

There are more people unemployed in the twenty-six counties than there are working in manufacturing industry.

●

American multinationals make their highest profits anywhere in the world, in Ireland.

●

In every area of the workforce women are concentrated in the lower, less skilled sectors. Outside the mainstream economy women's work is unpaid and devalued.

●

Only 17% of those trained by AnCO in 1984 were women. Temporary youth and employment schemes show a high level of segregation of women into restricted schemes.

●

More and more of our income goes in personal taxation — we now spend more on taxation than on food.

●

The catholic church owns property worth about £100 million in the Dublin area alone.

●

The national debt now stands at £20,000 million; all the income tax taken in by government in one year goes straight out again as interest payments on this debt.

●

Each time the dollar climbs by one cent against the Irish punt, it adds £35 million to the cost of Ireland's foreign interest payment.

●

61% of the price of a litre of petrol is tax.

●

The salaries of the thirty TDs who make up the government amounts to more than one million pounds each year.

●

The average income of a T.D. is about £17,000 — a single person on unemployment assistance gets about £1665 per year.

1
An Economy in Crisis

Foreign Profits, Foreign Debt

The economy of the twenty-six counties is in a state of severe crisis: over 240,000 people are unemployed; over one-third of the population is dependent on welfare; penal taxation levels cut people's earned income in half; government expenditure on critical services like health and education is being cut back.

The problem is not caused by a lack of resources: land, minerals and marine resources are abundant, and there is a young, growing and well-educated population. So what are the reasons for this crisis?

One reason is that much of the wealth being generated in the economy is being siphoned out. Multinational companies repatriate billions of pounds in profits from Irish subsidiaries every year. Furthermore, the country's own debt repayments are crippling, and a large proportion of our very high income taxes is used simply to pay the interest on the foreign debt built up over the last decade.

Instead of pumping money out of the country, it should be used to develop our own resources. We are becoming more and more dependent on food imports, and fishing and forestry are almost completely neglected. Norwegians establish fish farms here; our furniture industry imports timber; grain and paper are shipped in; essential industries have been lost as firm after firm closes down.

Of course, there are always those who thrive, even in an economic crisis. This country is rich in land speculators, money-makers and money-spinners. Those who pay for the crisis are the low-paid, those on welfare, the elderly, the redundant workers, the collapsed small businesses. Others double their profits, foreclose on debts, take over companies, move their investments abroad, speculate on currency and drive state cars.

Disappearing Profits

Over £1000 million worth of profits was taken out of this country by multinationals in 1985 alone. This is wealth generated by Irish workers, scarcely taxed and repatriated to America, Britain and Japan at a rapidly increasing pace. Resources for investment are lacking precisely because disappearing profits

and interest on the foreign debt pushes this country into a spiral of impoverishment and underdevelopment. No economy can develop in the interests of its people when its wealth and resources are drained to fill the bank accounts of powerful companies in other countries. Low investment, squandering of our natural resources, short-lived employment, cut-backs in government expenditure — this picture is directly connected to the national scandal of profit repatriation.

Between 1980 and 1985 £4034 million in profits was taken out of this country by multinational companies.

Despite the IDAs claims that multinationals reinvest their profits in this country, over 80% of multinational profits are taken out of this country as fast as they can move them.

The rate of profit being made by multinational companies located in Ireland is extremely high. The US department of commerce details the performance of US companies worldwide. Their own records show that **US companies make their highest profit rate in the world in Ireland.** Their rate of profit was over 30% in 1983, since then it fell slightly to just under 30%. A rate of profit of

The amount of profits taken out every year has been rising at a phenomenal rate since 1980. The estimate for repatriated profits that year was £258 million. For 1985, the figure was over £1300 million.

Year	Gross profit outflow	% change on previous year
1980	£258 million	
1981	£362 million	+40%
1982	£499 million	+38%
1983	£659 million	+32%
1984	£940 million	+43%
1985	£1316 million	+42%
Total	£4034 million	

30% means that the cost of investment is recovered in a period of just **three years.** Because a substantial proportion of that investment cost is actually raised in Ireland (IDA grants and bank loans), investment costs can be paid off in even less than three years and it is not long before profit rates are sky high. In marked contrast, a report by the Irish Management Institute in 1985 estimated that profit margins had fallen as low as 1% for Irish firms.

At the moment, Irish export trade seems to be doing well. For the first time, the amount we export is greater than the amount we import. Unfortunately, this is only a boom on paper. The main industries affected by the export boom are electronics and chemicals, and it is these same sectors who take their profit **out** of Ireland. John McMahon, the chief economist of the IDA, estimates that 85% of profits leaving the country are from the electronics and chemical industries.

So in practice the export boom makes little difference to the health of the economy, because export earnings do not stay here. They disappear out the other side as fast as they are made. Profits for other people are our chief export.

Mobile foreign investment is not the basis on which to build a stable economy. The industrial policy which was adopted in this country twenty-five years ago has created an economy of dependent development. High-tech companies set up here for a number of

JUST A LITTLE
SOMETHING I
PICKED UP IN
EUROPE

years, making incredible rates of profit, most of which they take out of the country. Our economy is like a shell, fragile and empty, all form and no content, short-term and short-sighted. Irish workers generate enormous wealth for others. This country is a dependent exploited link in an international chain, an attractive hunting ground on the periphery of Europe.

The Debt Treadmill

The other main route money takes out of this country is via the national debt. This now stands at £20,000 million. Over half of this huge debt is owed to foreign bankers, and the rest is owed to banks and individuals within this economy. This debt has accumulated over the years as successive governments have relied on borrowing to finance their expenditure. The interest payments are enormous, acting as a massive drain on the wealth and resources of the economy. The burden of the debt is shouldered by PAYE workers. As unemployment rises, the tax burden on those remaining in the paid workforce rises proportionately.

The total value of ALL the income tax collected by the government goes straight out again as interest payments on the national debt.

This does not mean that we are paying off the debt. This is what they call 'servicing the debt'. The cost of **interest payments** on the national debt came to £1900 million in 1984. The total value of revenue taken in income tax amounted to £1966 million in that same year.

Those in paid employment in this country number 1.1 million. The national debt works out at £5714 per head of the population or £18,182 for every worker. The national debt is a major cause of the high taxes, which make wages and salaries less and less valuable year by year.

Foreign Debt

Until the 1970s governments borrowed internally, from the people. Government issued bonds which anyone with ready cash could buy. The foreign bankers entered the picture over the last fifteen years. In 1964, the total amount paid out as interest to foreign bankers was only £1 million. Twenty years later in 1984 over £700 million was paid in interest to foreign bankers. About half of government borrowings is now from abroad. The foreign debt increased **five times** in the period from 1979 (when it was £1.5 billion) to 1985 (when it stood at £8.4 billion). State-sponsored bodies also borrow from foreign bankers adding a further £2 billion to the foreign debt. The total foreign debt now stands at £10.394 billion.

The American Connection

Most of the government's foreign borrowing is in dollars. Of the £10 billion government-owned foreign debt:

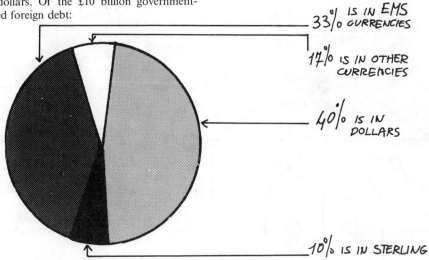

33% IS IN EMS CURRENCIES

17% IS IN OTHER CURRENCIES

40% IS IN DOLLARS

10% IS IN STERLING

Borrowing in dollars has become a characteristic of government borrowing over the last six years, so naturally the state of the Irish economy is extremely vulnerable to the changing value of the dollar. The value of the dollar went up rapidly between 1979 and 1984, making dollar-borrowing an expensive business. The depreciation of the Irish pound since 1979 has further increased the level of foreign debt, though this situation has eased off over recent months. However, any future increase in the value of the dollar relative to the punt will send the debt spiralling out of control.

Each time the dollar climbs by ONE CENT against the Irish pound, it adds £3.5 MILLION to the cost of Ireland's foreign interest payments.

In 1983, the rising value of the dollar added £495 million to the foreign debt, and a further £480 million was added in 1984. Over just two years almost £1 billion was added to the foreign debt **without any extra borrowing taking place.** So without anything happening in this country, the foreign debt of this economy can get hiked up in a stroke as international bankers buy and sell dollars. There's a lot you can do with £1 billion. You could run the entire health service of this country, employing 58,000 people.

The foreign debt is a **never-ending spiral.** Anyone who has paid back on a hire purchase agreement or house mortgage knows the score. A house loan of £30,000 actually costs £90,000 in total repayments over twenty-five years. Government borrowing today is at least partly to pay interest on yesterday's borrowing. That is the cycle. The foreign bankers are doing us no favours.

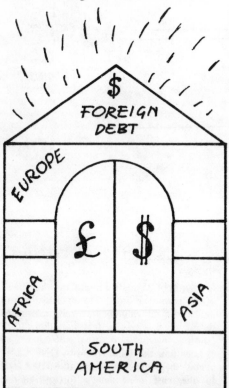

The foreign debt here is even higher than in countries like Brazil, Argentina and Mexico, although debt problems in South America make world headlines. It has been stated that if South America alone refused to pay, the international banking system would collapse. Yet, Ireland's credit rating remains high.

The foreign bankers have no intention of pulling the plug. **Euromoney** assesses credit ratings of each country every year. **Political stability** is as important as economic performance in drawing up such credit ratings. For the moment, the foreign bankers are content with the political and economic system in the twenty-six counties. Ireland rated twenty-third out of 112 countries in last year's **Euromoney.** (The US got the top rating, followed by West Germany, Japan and Britain). Like all loan sharks the foreign bankers don't want us to pay off the debt. **They want us to keep paying.** Year in and year out. The debt treadmill grinds on.

Work in the Mainstream Economy

Over the past sixty years a fundamental change has taken place in the nature of work in this country. The proportion of the workforce who are self-employed has shrunk, while paid employment has become the norm. About half the workforce made a living from small businesses, shops and farms in 1926, but only a quarter of the workforce is in this position today. While some sectors of the economy have become more important than others as a source of employment, the actual number at work in the formal economy has hardly changed over the last fifty years.

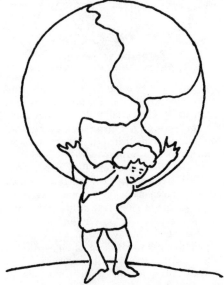

The nature of employment has undergone another dramatic change through the economic crisis of the last ten years. A job for life has become a thing of the past. Specialised skills have disappeared from the job market. Job turnover puts older workers in a particularly vulnerable position. Even in the public sector, the tradition of the permanent and pensionable job has been shaken to its roots by the closure of Irish Shipping, and in any case the virtual ban on recruitment in the public sector means that that kind of employment is simply not there for those coming onto the job market.

Getting into the workforce is no easy matter. There are far more unemployed people today than there are working in manufacturing industry. Young people find it difficult to get the experience now required for so many jobs in a shrinking labour market. Lack of childcare facilities, training and scarcity of employment opportunities restrict women's access to the workplace. The prevailing patriarchal attitude that 'a woman's place is in the home' is given much more of a voice during times of recession.

Unemployment is no longer a temporary problem. It is both widespread and permanent. As a result, more and more people are establishing and **investing their own money** in the setting up of co-operatives and small businesses of various kinds. On some streets, second-hand shops and small cafés seem to come and go with amazing speed, though state support for such enterprises is rarely forthcoming, and the banks are quick to foreclose. Yet state ideology is moving steadily closer to a position which presents employment as an 'individual problem', solved through self-help rather than a direct responsibility of the state.

Women on Local Employment Initiatives

The term Local Employment Initiatives (LEIs) has been coined to cover a wide variety of activities and enterprises, self managed companies, cooperatives; community businesses and other collective forms of working which are locally based and usually, though not always, small (less than 10-15 people). LEIs have become a movement composed of those who have decided to take action at local level to combat unemployment. Whilst they have gone unnoticed 'officially' until recently, LEIs are now becoming part of the economic and employment picture in most OECD (Organisation for Economic Cooperative Development) countries. In the EEC alone, the number of people employed in co-operatives has nearly doubled over the past five years. LEIs are non-traditional, innovative and are found mainly in the service sector. It is no coincidence that the growth in LEIs over the past decade has not only coincided with the rising problem of unemployment and its resulting poverty, but also the fact that women have been hit harder by unemployment than men. But there are other facts which have not

been sufficiently highlighted, such as the increased number of single parents; the number of divorces/separations has escalated as well as the number of families and couples

I'M READY TO LAY OFF THE WHOLE DAMN GOVERNMENT

living together who have not declared themselves 'officially' to the relevant authorities.

On an international scale statistics show that as women's social position changes, so too does their participation in the economy. The number of women who are sole supporters of themselves and their families has doubled over the last decade. However over 50 of women maintaining families, who were employed at any given time during 1980, were also living below the poverty line. The comparable rate for men was 14%.

Due to their social designation as women 'deemed dependent or as having dependan's', women encounter major discrimination in national enterprise schemes and social welfare schemes. The new family is more precarious and changing trends in the family means more women have to find jobs and new ways of employment. Necessity being the mother of invention — hence the growth of LEIs.

Although LEIs bear a passing resemblance to other small and medium sized enterprises, they differ because they are mostly set up by people who are unemployed or threatened with unemployment and are thus usually under-capitalised at the outset. Although they seek to be viable businesses, jobs are their primary objective.

Where do people work?

Statistics on employment refer only to the 'official' workforce. Unpaid work is not measured by such data. Women working in the home, voluntary workers and many others are not included. There are also thousands of casual workers, outworkers and contract workers who never appear on the records.

The following table gives a breakdown of the total numbers at work in the different areas of the official economy in 1984:

Area of economy	Numbers	%
Mining, quarrying & turf	10,000	0.9
Manufacturing industries	212,000	19.1
Building & construction	83,000	7.5
Electricity, gas and water	15,000	1.3
Commerce, insurance & finance	212,000	19.1
Transport & communications	69,000	6.2
Public administration and defence	73,000	6.6
Other (non-agricultural)	254,000	22.9
Agriculture, forestry and fishing	182,000	16.4
Total	1,110,000	100.0
Numbers out of work:	231,000	17% (July 1985)

Another way of looking at this information, using a more general breakdown, would give the following picture:

Sector of economy	% of labour force
Industry	27%
Agriculture	16%
Services	57%

Manufacturing Industry

There are nearly 200,000 people employed in manufacturing industries in the twenty-six counties. About one in five (20%) of these are women. In June 1985 the workforce statistics broke down like this:

Manufacturing sector	Employment
Metals & engineering	58,700
Food	37,400
Clothing, footwear & leather	15,100
Non-metallic minerals	12,700
Paper & printing	12,600
Chemicals	12,100
Textiles	11,100
Wood & furniture	8,700
Drink & tobacco	8,700
Miscellaneous industries	10,100
Total	187,200

Employment in manufacturing industry increased during the 1960s and 1970s, mainly due to the large number of multinational companies who set up subsidiaries here during those years. The Lemass government at that time, adopted a policy of opening up the economy to foreign investment, following the deep depression and mass emigration of the fifties. Protectionism, a policy that had been pursued in the thirties, was based on developing native industry and keeping imports out by imposing tariffs and other legislation. This policy was now declared a 'failure', and the new industrial policy radically altered the ownership of industry in this country.

Of the top 1000 companies in the economy, 47% are foreign controlled. Over one-third of the entire manufacturing workforce works for multinational companies. Traditionally Irish-owned industries are clothing, footwear, textiles, leatherwork, food and engineering. The labour-intensive clothing and footwear

sectors, which have a high percentage of women employed, have been particularly badly hit by the recession. Growth has been confined to those sectors where foreign ownership is dominant, such as electronics, pharmaceuticals and chemicals.

Since 1981, employment in manufacturing industry has been falling consistently. New factories opening up have not kept pace with the rate of closure and job loss. Hundreds of millions have been paid out in grants and incentives to entice multinational companies to set up shop. Many of these new plants stay in place for a few years and then move on. About one-third of the multinational companies which set up in this country leave within ten years of opening. 20,000 jobs were lost in multinational companies between 1973 and 1981 alone. Many of these companies were located in rural areas or small towns and became a focal point for the development of the local economy. Closure of such companies has a devastating impact on employment in a whole area.

Multinational subsidiaries in the economy are concentrated in a few key sectors. They generally import materials and equipment and export the final product. Manufacturing industry has become tied into the international economy, producing less and less for home consumption.

Percentage of foreign firms in manufacturing sectors	%
Chemicals	62%
Metals & engineering	58%
Textiles	35%
Drink & tobacco	35%
Clothing & footwear	26%
Non-metallic minerals	16%
Food	14%
Paper & printing	9%

Workers in these industries are often engaged in carrying out one small task in an international production process. Irish workers often never see the full product they are working on. They work on a **global assembly line.** Production is broken up into separate pieces, some located in Singapore, others in California and one part in Ireland.

Multinational companies in the Irish economy use this country as an **operations base.** Their main objective is to get access to the EEC markets and also to benefit from the extremely generous tax relief and grants available from the Industrial Development Authority (IDA).

There are over 850 subsidiaries of multinationals in the twenty-six counties. The greatest number are American in origin.

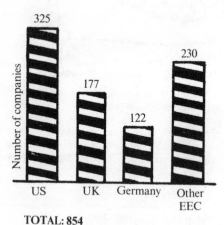

TOTAL: 854

Grants and Incentives

The system of grants and tax incentives available for new companies setting up in the twenty-six counties is one of the most attractive packages anywhere in the world. The majority of these benefits go to foreign companies, who lay out little by way of investment funds when they set up here. Two-thirds of the investment money is made up of IDA grants and other capital raised through the banking sector and elsewhere in the Irish economy. In other words, two-thirds of the investment cost of setting up a subsidiary is drawn from the Irish economy, while ownership and control remain under the parent company in another country.

The vast proportion of the grants paid out to new and expanding industries setting up in this country between 1979 and 1983 went to foreign companies. £421 million went to Irish companies while £1183 million went to foreign companies. **In all, 64% of all capital grants during those years went to foreign companies.** Despite an emphasis on small industry in recent years, grants still tend to go to export-oriented, large-scale, capital-intensive industry.

Manufacturing industry as a whole is subject to a maximum tax on profits of 10%. This is an extremely low rate of taxation. In other sectors of the economy, such as construction and services, the tax rate runs as high as 50%. Manufacturers receive other generous tax concessions, against capital investment and depreciation. To quote the IDA, which administers grants to industry:

In all parts of the country, a company can depreciate 100% of the total cost of fixed plant, machinery and buildings and write it off against tax — and in the first year if they wish.

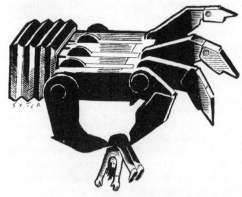

The Grants

Non-repayable cash grants worth between 45% and 60% of the total fixed asset costs of setting up a new company are available. This grant covers plant, equipment and machinery and makes establishing a company a cheap and simple operation. These grants act as a 'subsidy to capital' in that they are calculated on the basis of the **value of the investment** rather than on the numbers employed.

Research and development grants are also available and they amount to as much as 50% of the cost of an approved project or a ceiling of £250,000, whichever is greater.

Training grants are paid out by the IDA to the value of 100% of the cost of agreed training programmes for workers in new industries.

These grants can cover the cost of sending employees abroad, their salaries, training costs and subsistence.

Technology acquisition grants can be claimed by companies who are modernising their plant and production process through the introduction of new technology.

Low interest-rate loans are also available from the banking sector whereby the banks avail of a wealth of tax concessions by leasing equipment and machinery to the company and offering special low interest loans in exchange.

The IDA provides the buildings for many new companies through its **advance factory programme** under which it constructs factories in different parts of the country and then leases or sells these on very favourable terms to the company. The decrease in new investment over the past few years has left many of these factories vacant.

The average cost of a job under the IDA system (including both grants and administration) is about £20,000. Their budget of about £250 million in an average year produces around 11,000 new jobs. But job loss has been relentless. Over the last five years job losses have been greater than the number of new jobs created.

It is ironical to note that even though, on an international level, the service industries are recognised as the largest potential growth areas, in Ireland the government refuses to offer any support to the developing service sector. For example the publishing industry which directly supports printing, designated as manufacturing, is not eligible for any of the supports listed above. The statistics containing quotes by the IDA that only 5% of those who approach them are women can now be seen in its proper context.

Wages in manufacturing

There are huge differences in the average earnings of women and men in manufacturing industry, despite the fact that some of the growth areas, for example electronics and health-care products, employ mainly women workers. In March 1984, the average hourly rate for women workers in manufacturing

" OH! THAT EXPLAINS THE DIFFERENCE IN OUR WAGES "

industry was £2.86 — the male hourly rate was £4.49. On a weekly basis, women take home an average of £106.86, while men workers take home on average £176.15. While it is true that the length of the working week for men (42.1 hours) is longer than for women 37.4 hours) there is still a significant gap in earnings.

Average earnings vary widely from sector to sector.

PICKING UP THE PIECES: A WOMEN'S RESOURCE PACK.

For women workers, pay is lowest in the clothing, textiles and wood and furniture industries. Those same industries also pay the lowest male rates. The highest rates prevail in those industries which employ predominantly male workers. At the extreme ends of the scale, average female earnings in the clothing and footwear industry are £88.80 a week while male earnings in the chemical industry average out at £227.98 a week. Wage levels in this country are generally low compared to most other EEC countries, particularly when comparisons of **take-home pay** are made.

Work in Agriculture

Traditionally agriculture was the major source of employment and income in the twenty-six counties. Today only 16% of the workforce, a total of 182,000 people, are employed in the agricultural sector.

Male workers in agriculture tend to be the only ones 'officially' recognised as working the land. Women who work on family farms rarely appear in statistics. Thousands of women are classified as 'relatives assisting' on the farm. Statistically, this is not calculated as a full job. Only those women who own and run their own farms are considered to be farmers. As a result, only 6% of farmers are female in official records.

Within the agricultural sector there are enormous differences in farming conditions, farm size and income. On the one hand, there is the commercial sector — large farms mainly involved in dairy farming and tillage. At the other end of the scale, there are the small farms with poor land mainly involved in drystock production. Between these two lie the bulk of middle size farms often combining different kinds of farming and covering a range of different income levels. The following table shows the breakdown of farms by size:

Number of acres	% of farms
1-25	31%
25-50	30%
50-150	30%
150+	9%

The majority of farms (61%) are under 50 acres. The small size of many farms, combined with poor land and type of farming means that farm income is often abysmally low.

Farm Income

30% of all full-time farmers live on an income from the farm of less than £3000 a year. The average income from dairy farming is more than treble the average income from drystock farming.

Farm income (per year)	% of farms
0-£3000	30%
£3000-£6000	27%
£6000+	43%

The lowest farm incomes are, not surprisingly, in Ulster (62% of the national average) and Connaught (50% of the national average). In Ulster 75% of farms are less than 50 acres and in Connaught 79% are less than 50 acres. These circumstances have forced a growing number of farmers to become part-time farmers seeking out scarce employment opportunities outside the farm while continuing to work the land.

Emigration

A steady stream of emigration from rural Ireland, particularly during the 1950s, has created a situation of virtual depopulation in some rural areas. Emigration was exceptionally high among young women who left for the cities and for other countries in search of work. As a result, there is a very high proportion of elderly single farmers without relatives to pass the land to. The average age of small farmers, part-time farmers and retired farmers is very high.

unavailable. Traditionally, land was passed through the male line, but contemporary conditions in rural Ireland have undermined this blatantly discriminatory social system.

EEC Agricultural Policy

Membership of the EEC has had a very uneven impact on Irish farmers. The EEC agricultural policy is known as the CAP (Common Agricultural Policy). The CAP includes two major kinds of subsidies to agriculture: grants for development and guaranteed prices for produce.

Category of farmer	% of all farmers	Average age
Small farmers	22%	60 years
Part-time farmers	23%	45 years
Retired/semi-retired farmers	10%	70 years

One of the consequences of this situation is that it is extremely difficult for young people to enter farming. Land is expensive and often

Farm Modernisation Scheme

The primary grants scheme from the EEC is the Farm Modernisation Scheme (FMS). Under this scheme, each farm for which a grant is applied is classified under one of three headings. These categories are based on their current or potential ability to generate an income equal to the average industrial wage. The three categories are:

Commercial: those farms which generate an income equal to or above the average industrial wage.

Development: those who have the potential to generate such an income over a period of six to eight years.

Other: those farms which are assessed as not in a position to generate such an income — in EEC terms such farms are not viable and their farmers are destined eventually to leave agriculture.

EEC Price System (Intervention)

In addition to the grant system administered under the Farm Modernisation Scheme, the EEC **guarantees** prices for agricultural produce. Target prices are set for various agricultural products by the EEC council of agricultural ministers. Such prices are then maintained by the system of **intervention:** if market prices fall too far below the target price the EEC intervenes and buys up produce which is then stored. This process creates an artificially high demand for the product, forcing the price to move up towards the target price.

In 1984, 30% of the total agricultural produce of the EEC was held in storage. This is where the butter, beef, wine and grain mountains come from. This system of guaranteeing prices using intervention has also benefited Irish farmers in an uneven way. The more you produce the more you get in the form of price supports. The larger, more 'productive' farms, get the greatest income injection through this system.

A serious consequence of EEC membership is the high prices we all end up paying in the shops for food and food products. Consumer prices have trebled since 1973. This means hardship for those on welfare and low incomes.

Only farms which come under the category of 'commercial' or 'development' are eligible for the full grants under the FMS.

Most Irish farmers received no benefit from the grants scheme after they were categorised in December 1982. Out of a total of 223,500 farms only 26% were classified as 'development' farms and a further 4% as 'commercial farms'. Over half (57%) of the grants available under the FMS went to these two categories. Together, they represent only 30% of the Irish farming community. Only 10% of those with farms of 50 acres or less have been eligible for this scheme.

In some areas of the country, such as Connaught and Ulster where land is relatively poor, the percentage of 'development' or 'commercial' farms is tiny: 8% in Connaught and 15% in Ulster. By contrast, in Munster and Leinster 'development' or 'commercial' farms are more numerous: 38% in Munster and 39% in Leinster. Since the FMS was introduced, nearly £300 million has been paid out to Irish farmers, but it has been of little benefit to the majority of Irish farmers.

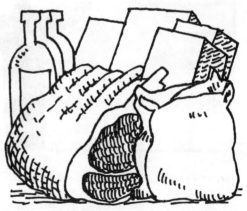

There is mounting opposition within the EEC to the CAP. Britain and West Germany in particular (the industrial lobby) oppose continuation of the guaranteed prices system.

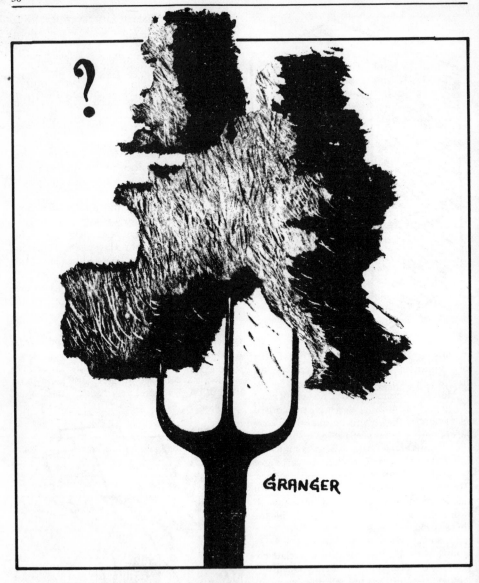

GRANGER

The cost of such extensive storage of produce is a critical factor here. Already, the EEC has begun to limit by **quotas** the output levels of those agricultural products where intervention has been consistently relied on. They have already limited the output of milk and other produce within the EEC. Irish farmers' organisations are vehemently opposed to such developments.

These moves in the EEC are acting as an incentive to some enterprising farmers to investigate the possibilities of a more mixed approach to farming, exploring new crops and examining the potential of horticulture. Over

90% of our land is under pasture, used for grazing both drystock and dairy cattle. To this day, **less than 6%** of the major natural resource, a fertile soil, is used for the growing of crops. The result of this is that while the agricultural system is oriented towards the export market, the economy remains dependent on importing £850 million worth of food every year, including potatoes. Most of the vegetables we eat are imported.

The great majority of our agricultural produce is exported out of this country **without being processed.** Cattle are generally exported live. Processing of milk into milk products continues to operate on a very limited scale, confined to butter, hard cheeses and milk powder. As a result, the number of people employed in the food industry is falling, while food imports dominate the home market.

EEC membership has not oriented our agricultural system towards a longer-term, more creative strategy. On the contrary, it has meant a short-term injection of cash to one section of those employed on the land. Instead of developing towards an economy self-sufficient in food, with a strong export market, we have become more dependent on food imports and subsidised farm produce.

Services Sector

There are over half a million service workers in the economy. Services employ about three-quarters of all women workers and about half of all male workers. Service employment was the growth area of the 1970s. The most important employers are the public sector, banks, insurance companies, retail outlets (shops and restaurants) and the professions. Conditions of work vary enormously in the services sector.

If we look at the breakdown of employment among men and women of different age groups, the importance of the services sector is evident.

1984	Men			Women		
	15-19	**20-24**	**25+**	**15-19**	**20-24**	**25+**
Total industry	39%	38%	32%	26%	24%	15%
Commerce, insurance, finance & business	25%	21%	16%	29%	26%	20%
Transport, communications and storage	3%	6%	8%	2%	5%	4%
Professions	10%	7%	10%	17%	24%	36%
Public administration & defence	3%	10%	6%	3%	9%	5%
Other	6%	5%	4%	20%	11%	11%
Total services	47%	49%	45%	72%	75%	77%
All industries	100%	100%	100%	100%	100%	100%
Numbers	46,300	100,900	623,400	38,100	93,500	207,600

Over 300,000 of those working in services work in the public sector. The health and education services are the most important areas of public service employment.

1983	
Civil service	37,000
Police	10,800
Defence forces	16,500
Local authorities	31,900
Health services	58,900
Education	51,600
State-sponsored bodies	95,100
Total	301,800

Women are more heavily concentrated in service employment than men, across all age groups. Nearly half of those working in government departments are women while other service occupations show an even higher concentration of women workers:

69% of personal service workers are women
59% of professional service workers are women
72% of primary education workers are women
70% of hospital workers are women
57% of catering workers are women

Predictably, women occupy the lower end of the occupational scale in services as elsewhere. Only 5% of administrative, executive and managerial workers are female.

The service industry does not qualify for IDA grants unless 90% of its business is for export purposes. The government in this country has refused to offer any real support to developing small industries in the services sector.

Service employment is one of the few areas of work that has a real potential for decentralisation. Much service employment is small-scale. Every town and village has its pubs, post offices, shops and cafés. At government level, there has been little attempt to develop this

potential. However, Nuala Fennell, Minister of State for Womens Affairs, recognising this gap has launched her own programme for 'women in business'. However, this still leaves this area grossly underfunded, a situation that discriminates directly against women. Public-sector jobs are Dublin-centred. The mass exodus from Dublin on buses and trains every Friday evening demonstrates a real lack of forethought and planning. Coming to Dublin for work is a necessity not a choice. Many of those on the weekend trail are working in the banks and public services, sectors which could easily be extensively decentralised.

Traditionally a labour-intensive area of employment, new technology is turning inside out the whole area of 'white collar' work. Capital investment in services, evident in the huge array of new equipment becoming familiar in modern offices, is designed to increase the speed and productivity of service work.

Electronic technology cuts through mounds of paper and filing, allowing instantaneous transmission of information without recourse to the physical movement of paper. The consequence is a serious reduction in jobs, which some commentators have predicted to run to between 25% and 45% of current employment levels. This development means that women workers will find it even more difficult to get jobs.

Women in the Workforce

Women are particularly affected by the way in which the official workforce is calculated. There are countless ways in which women's work is regarded as non-existent, because it is 'invisible'. Unpaid domestic labour is the most important of these, but women are also the invisible workforce in voluntary organisations, in the community, on the farm and in the unrecorded, heavily exploited areas of casual work.

Even so, the numbers of women in the 'official' workforce have been increasing over the past decade, despite the severe unemployment crisis. It is among married women in the over twenty-five age group that this increase has been most evident.

Just over 36% of women aged fifteen to sixty-four are part of the labour force of the mainstream economy. The following table gives a breakdown of the principal economic status of women.

Economic status	Numbers of women (aged 15-64)	% women
At work	331,900	32%
Unemployed	46,500	4%
Student	116,800	11%
On home duties	526,100	50%
Other	20,400	2%
Total	1041,800	100%

Although more married women are joining the workforce, nearly 60% of women workers are single, and the majority are under thirty years of age. In all, just over 30% of the recorded workforce (339,100) is female. The concentration of women workers in the services is seen in the following table:

Women at Work Classified by Industrial Group

	Number	% of total persons
Agriculture, forestry & fishing	19,000	10%
Manufacturing industry	57,600	27%
Other industry	4,900	4%
Wholesale distribution	8,500	19%
Retail distribution	49,000	40%
Insurance, finance & business	20,500	47%
Transport, communication & storage	13,800	20%
Public administration & defence	21,000	29%
Professional services	102,500	57%
Personal services	36,800	64%
Other groups	5,300	32%
Total	**339,100**	**31%**

Within manufacturing, women workers are concentrated in the traditional clothing, footwear and textile sectors and the newer electronics and health-care products industries. Women workers are segregated into particular areas of the workforce and also into particular occupations. Within the professions, women work mainly as nurses and teachers, the lower-paid end of the spectrum of professional work. The great bulk of women workers are concentrated in the clerical area. Banking, insurance and retail services provide the other major sources of female employment.

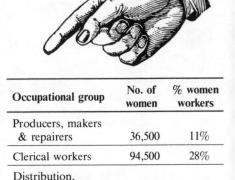

Occupational group	No. of women	% women workers
Producers, makers & repairers	36,500	11%
Clerical workers	94,500	28%
Distribution, insurance and finance workers	43,900	13%
Service workers	48,100	14%
Professional & technical workers	81,600	24%
Total	**339,100**	**100%**

The concentration of women workers in service employment means that women are particularly vulnerable to the intense rationalisation of work taking place there. Capital investment in office work, the retail/distribution and commerce/insurance/finance sectors means a reduction in employment opportunities as they move away from labour-intensive work processes. Already, the banks and the public sector have seriously cut down on recruitment at a time when the numbers of women seeking access to paid employment is growing.

Over the past fifteen years it has been in clerical, professional and technical work that the greatest increase in the numbers of women workers has been recorded.

Women at Work by Occupational Group

Occupational group	1971	1981	% change
Clerical workers	65,252	97,177	+49%
Professional & technical workers	49,924	73,544	+47%
Producers, makers & repairers	43,333	40,924	−6%
Service workers	46,969	47,691	+2%
Distribution, insurance & finance	34,659	40,114	+16%
Other occupations	12,398	16,625	−34%
TOTAL	**252,535**	**316,007**	**+25%**

The critical issue for women workers is that in **both** the areas where employment for women has increased over the past fifteen years, current developments indicate a reversal of this trend. In the clerical area, job opportunities are shrinking as new electronic technologies spread through this sector, while in the area of professional work, cutbacks in public expenditure are concentrated in the education and health services, the main sources of employment for women professional workers.

A further look at the data from the 1971 and 1981 census of population reinforces this pattern.

Women at Work
Outside of Agriculture in
1971 and 1981 Classified by Industry

	1971	1981	% change
Manufacturing industries	65,370	63,778	-2%
Wholesale & retail distribution	46,123	55,138	+20%
Insurance, finance & business services	9,608	20,367	+112%
Transport, communication & storage	9,533	13,301	+40%
Public administration & defence	11,547	20,628	+79%
Professional services	37,694	34,329	-9%
Other industries & services	8,140	11,197	+38%
Total	**252,535**	**316,007**	**+25%**

What emerges so clearly from this table is that insurance, banking and the public sector have been key growth areas for female employment. Precisely in the areas that employment opportunities peaked, they are now falling. Employment opportunities for women workers are shrinking rapidly.

State Employment Schemes

During the last five years, there has been an explosion in all kinds of state schemes designed to provide temporary employment to different categories of the unemployed. Over 20,000 people are participating in various state schemes. Some of them are confined to people under twenty-five years, others to those over twenty-five. Such schemes involve a minimal amount of training or real work experience. They are **the** growth area of the labour market. They only rarely turn into long-term employment opportunities. The following table is a breakdown of the numbers participating in such schemes in June 1985.

Although women make up over half of those attending these schemes, there is a strong pattern of sex segregation running through the system. Women are confined to an extremely narrow range of schemes reinforcing sex stereotyping on the labour market. For example, women make up 99% of the participants on secretarial courses and only 10% of those on the Enterprise Allowance Scheme. So, while entry requirements discriminate against women with children, women who do manage to get on these schemes are channelled into restricted programmes.

Participants on selected State Employment Training Schemes 1984

	Total	% Women
Work Experience Programme	3833	64%
Teamwork	1200	45%
Environmental Works Scheme	390	1%
Pre-Employment Scheme	4270	30%
Secretarial	7082	99%
Farm Training	1855	3%
Enterprise Allowance Scheme	2749	10%
Other	416	25%

Most of the support schemes on offer are not available to the majority of women due to social welfare classifications and discrimination. Through economic necessity or choice many more women are now returning to the workforce without the support of many of the State schemes on offer to other sectors of the community. It should also be noted that for most women's and community groups payments from these schemes are made retrospectively causing further financial difficulty.

Employment Incentive Scheme

Under this scheme a subsidy is paid to **employers** (excluding banks and public sector) who take on up to two additional workers off the 'live register' of the unemployed. £30 a week is paid for one worker and £60 a week for two workers. (£60 a week may be paid for one worker officially defined as long-term unemployed.) This subsidy is available for six months and employment must last for at least this length of time. There is no age limit, but those employed must have been registered as unemployed for at least thirteen weeks. The trade unions have consistently attacked this scheme as a source of cheap labour for employers, without any guarantee of real training.

Enterprise Allowance Scheme

This scheme is based on encouraging self-employment among those on the live register, or those who have come off disability benefit or off an approved training course. The successful applicant gets £30 a week for **one year** (£50 for a married person) while they attempt to generate income as self-employed. Any area of economic activity is eligible, except 'gaming' or the promotion of political or religious views. Applicants must show they can invest £500 from their own resources in the business if deemed necessary. No applicant can reapply for a second run of this scheme. The strictness of this eligibility criteria means that many women, including those who have just completed an approved training course, are not eligible. Women who have been working in the home and/or bringing up children are not entitled to unemployment benefit or assistance because they are outside the 'paid' workforce. In the case of a mother with young children she is not considered *available* for work, 'her place is at home with *her* children, therefore she is not entitled to the dole. Unmarried mothers and deserted wives are also ineligible. Because they are in receipt of allowances and not unemployment payments they are not entitled to sign on. In effect the only women eligible for the Enterprise Allowance Scheme are single women without children.

Social Employment Scheme

This involves part-time work on 'projects of community value'. It is open only to those who have been on unemployment assistance for twelve months or more. Eligible projects must be non-commercial, 'respond to com-

munity needs', last at least four months and must not substitute for existing employment. Applicants should be over twenty-five years of age (although persons under twenty-five are not excluded). Again, this scheme effectively excludes women with children as applicants must be on unemployment assistance for a year.

Participants on this scheme are paid £70 a week for a two-and-a-half-day week. The Women's Advisory Committee of the Irish Congress of Trade Unions has opposed this scheme because of its discriminatory bias.

Teamwork Scheme

This involves full-time work on 'projects of community value' for unemployed young people aged seventeen to twenty-five years. Any voluntary non-profit-making organisation, which is considered to have 'social or

Derek Speirs (Report)

cultural objectives' (such as a youth or community group) can sponsor a teamwork project. Projects excluded from this scheme are those which involve 'private gain', those which could cause job displacement or which involve trading. Construction and training projects are also excluded as they are deemed

to be covered by other schemes. Projects must be for a minimum of six months and participants stay on a programme for a maximum of one year. A grant of £70 a week is available for each participant and every group of ten people will be managed by a supervisor on a £105 a week grant. Running costs up to a maximum of 15% of the total labour grants are also available.

Work Experience Programme

This is another youth programme, open only to those under twenty-five years. It is defined as a programme for the young unemployed to 'gain experience' that will help them in job seeking.

Each participant is paid £34.50 per week and goes through a six-month placement with public or private sector employers. This programme is administered by the National Manpower Service and involved around 4000 young people in 1984. This scheme can be used as a cheap means of maintaining employment levels. It can also prevent a proper job from being created.

Youth Schemes

State expenditure on the multitude of youth employment schemes amounted to an estimated £140 million in 1984. In that same year, youth employment was 'officially' 69,000. Of the £140 million spent in 1984, over half, or £83.25 million, came from the Youth Employment Levy. This is a 1% levy on all earned income, which is deducted at source from all those on wages and salaries and the self-employed. The rest of the budget came from the European Social Fund. The majority of this budget (£90 million) is allocated to training programmes organised under various state agencies: AnCO, CERT, and ACOT. About £18 million went to various temporary employment schemes, including employment subsidies going directly to employers. The rest of the budget, over £25 million, went to the department of education to fund pre-employment and secretarial courses.

The following table gives a breakdown of the numbers of young people who were involved in a range of state schemes during 1984.

Programme	No. of young people
Training	34,983
Work experience	8,504
Temporary work	7,865
Vocational education	12,377

AnCO was involved in the training programmes, both in its own training centres and under external training agencies, for about 21,000 young people in 1984. Other training programmes come under CERT (hotels and catering) and ACOT (farming certificate). In addition, the Community Youth Training Programme and Training for Travellers involved a further 15,000 young people.

Pre-employment courses are funded under the vocational education system. They act as an additional year within the school system before a young person enters the labour market or joins the dole queue. Of the 12,400 young people who attended such courses in 1984, the majority (7300) were on secretarial courses. Such a programme feeds into the office work area, where the long-term possibilities for employment opportunities are likely to be restricted as new technology spreads.

Criticism of the various employment schemes has focussed on their temporary nature and the lack of real skills gained under such projects. Many environmental projects, for example the cleaning of rivers and landscaping, as well as cultural projects (theatre and video) and community projects have been funded under these schemes. The result is often the build-up of energy, initiative and facilities which are undermined by the withdrawal of funding. Work experience projects can end up providing a source of cheap labour without enhancing the skills or work options of the unemployed.

These schemes often benefit the employer more than anyone else. A cheap, expendable workforce organised by the state is constantly on tap. Unionisation is virtually non-existent. There is the added advantage of keeping the unemployment figures down by an average 15,000 over a year. Every little helps.

Training

The major training agency in the twenty-six counties is AnCO, which had an annual budget of £100 million in 1984. Just over half of this budget comes from the European Social Fund, about 10% is a direct government grant and the other 40% from the Youth Employment Agency (YEA). AnCO has been increasingly relying on external training agencies in recent years, a system of contracting out training usually to private businesses. External training is the only way in which a community or women's project can get involved in training, but breaking the state monopoly is difficult. AnCO favours businesses like computer companies and rarely favours applications from co-operatives, for instance.

A total of 39,689 adults and apprentices went through the AnCO training programme over 1983/84, as the following table shows.

Adults trained in AnCO training centres	24,245
Adults trained by external training division	12,689
Apprentices trained in AnCO training centres	2,755
Total	39,689

Just over 8000 of those trained in 1984 were over twenty-five years of age, that is 20% of the total. The vast majority of trainees are male. **In 1984, only 17% of those undergoing AnCO training were women.** Training continues to be a male-dominated activity — only 6690 women were trained by AnCO in 1984, under its adult training programme. Generally, training is oriented towards **young men**. Training programmes often segregate male and female trainees, and certain courses are seen as female courses, while others tend to be almost exclusively male.

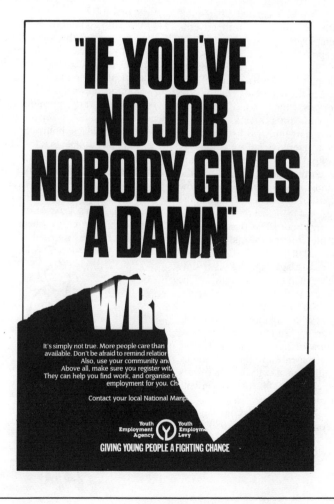

Part-Time and Casual Work

Most part-time and casual workers are women service workers. Part-time and casual employment is generally the lowest paid work in the economy. It is extremely insecure, low-status, and often unskilled work and it is not covered by protective labour legislation. Employment of this type has been increasing among women workers in both the six and the twenty-six counties, and in most European countries. There are eleven million part-time workers in Europe, of whom nine million are married women. As the recession intensified and unemployment levels escalated, part-time work has been promoted by both governments and employers as a new area of 'employment opportunity'.

One-third of all women workers in the six counties work part-time. Just over 16% of women workers in the twenty-six counties are part-time workers, but official data is extremely unreliable in this area as the casual nature of much part-time work excludes it from 'recorded' employment. In the six counties 84% of part-time women workers are married. The corresponding figure for the twenty-six counties is 75%, despite the still low rate of participation of married women in the paid workforce.

In all, there are about 120,000 women part-timers across the country (67,000 in the six counties and 53,000 in the twenty-six counties). The average age of part-time workers is higher than that of full-timers. The majority are over twenty-five years of age.

Women part-time workers are confined to a number of key occupations; shopwork, catering, cleaning and the professions. Women tend to work part-time as the number of their children increases. In the six counties, just over 40% of women with one child work part-time whereas over 70% of women with four children work part-time.

In a report for the Equal Opportunities Commission for the six counties 1983, Janet Trewsdale and Mary Trainor describe the part-time worker:

We can draw an identikit picture of the Northern Ireland part-time worker as being female, married, aged over 35, working in distributive trades or other services in a non or low skilled job with at least two dependent children at home.

In contrast to the position of women part-time workers, male part-timers tend to be very young and mainly in the catering industry. The spread of part-time work has drawn increasingly on younger workers, frequently in their first job.

Working conditions for part-timers reflect their position at the edges of the mainstream economy. Holiday pay, sick pay, redundancy settlements and contracts of employment are often denied to part-time workers.

Contract cleaners work for about £2 an hour during early mornings or late evenings and earn about £36 for an average working week of eighteen hours. State employment schemes pay double that for a two-and-a-half-day week, but exclude married women on the basis of criteria of eligibility (see last section).

Part-time teachers in the twenty-six counties get paid on an hourly basis with no provision for holidays, sick leave or redundancy and the absence of any employment contract means that they can be dismissed at an hour's notice.

The Taxation System

Tax revenue	Amount £ million	% of total
Income tax	2131	37%
Value-added tax	1484	26%
Excise duties	1317	23%
Corporation tax	219	4%
Motor tax	120	2%
Customs	105	2%
Youth employment levy	86	2%
Income levy	77	1%
Capital taxes	34	1%

Every state raises revenue through taxation. Tax revenue can be raised by taxing income, wealth, land, property or spending. The tax system in the twenty-six counties is based on heavily taxing two of these: regular income and spending. Those on fixed wages and salaries are heavily taxed on their regular incomes. But that isn't the end of it. Spending is also taxed: every time an item of adult clothing, a kitchen utensil or a magazine is bought, the government gets its cut.

Wealth taxation in this country is derisory. Every attempt to tax land, property and wealth has met with massive resistance from property owners. Only a minute portion of tax revenue comes from any source other than the PAYE (income tax deducted on the pay-as-you-earn system) systems and VAT (value-added tax) and excise duties. The following table shows the various sources of government revenue during 1985. The smallest item is capital taxation. Income tax, VAT and excise duties (the last two are both spending taxes) make up **86% of all taxation revenue.**

Personal Taxes

Personal taxes are taxes on personal income and personal spending and make up the **growing majority** of all taxation revenue. If income and expenditure taxes are combined, the government is taking **over one-third** of total wealth generated in the economy over one year through personal taxation. And this amount is increasing each year. The government take through taxation is rising **faster than inflation,** despite the much-heralded tax reforms of the 1986 budget. Personal taxation has risen from 12.2% of GNP in 1982 to 14.7% of GNP in 1986.

Taxes on **personal income** (income tax and the youth employment levy) are expected to yield £2477 million to government this year. This represents an **increase** of £217 million or 9.6% over last year. This increase is at least **three times higher** than the rate of inflation.

Expenditure taxation is also rising faster than inflation. The 'official' projected take for 1986 through taxes on spending is £3342 million or just 20% of GNP.

	(£ million)	
	1985	**1986**
Gross national product	15,670	16,825
Taxes on personal income	2,260	2,477
— As % of GNP	14.4%	14.7%
Taxes on personal spending	3,057	3,342
— As % of GNP	19.5%	19.9%
Total personal taxes as % of GNP	33.9%	34.6%

*excludes PRSI deductions.
1986 figures are 'official' projections.

Not everyone pays tax equally. The weight of the income tax burden is disproportionately borne by those on **fixed regular wages and salaries.** For the **individual** taxpayer on a regular fixed income, the proportion of income going on personal taxation is often as high as 60%. This is made up of deductions on income (income tax, PRSI, and the levy) averaging at 40% and a further 20% in deductions through taxation on spending. This is a conservative estimate.

We now spend more on income taxes than we spend on food.

In 1983, the personal tax take by the government amounted to £2665 million. In that same year the total amount spent on food in this country was £2258 million. In fact, 20% of income went on income tax, while only 17% of income was spent on food. The following table gives a detailed breakdown of household expenditure for 1983, the latest available data:

Distribution of Household Expenditure in 1983

Personal income & wealth tax	2,665	20%	
Personal saving	2,118	16%	
Personal spending	8,767	64%	
— food		2258	17%
— alcoholic drink		1044	8%
— tobacco		422	3%
— clothing & footwear		579	4%
— rent		544	4%
— fuel and power		522	4%
— household goods		594	4%
— transport & communication		1182	9%
— entertainment, education and recreation		844	6%
— other goods		805	6%
— spending abroad		363	3%
— less: spending by tourists		(−390)	(−3%)
Total personal income	**13,550**		**100%**

The table shows a total personal income of £13,550 million. 64% is actually **spent** on goods and services. **This expenditure is itself taxed.** In 1983, expenditure taxation amounted to £2651 million. 30% of this money spent on goods and services went back to the government in tax.

Amount Paid in Tax 1984	
PAYE sector	£1678 million
Self-employed	£255 million
Farmers	£33 million

Income Tax

Income tax is a major source of revenue to the state. Nearly 40% of all tax revenue comes from taxing income.

There are two ways of paying income tax: the PAYE system of deductions at source and the self-assessment system used by the self employed. The bulk of income tax comes from those caught in the PAYE net. The vast majority of wage and salary earners pay under the PAYE system (or schedule E), accounting for 78% of all taxpayers. The self-employed are taxed under schedule D, a system of recording all income earned during the year, subtracting tax allowances and business expenses and paying tax on the rest of your earnings.

PAYE workers paid 85% of all income taxes, but they make up only 78% of taxpayers and include the lowest paid among their ranks. For every £10 collected in income tax revenue in one year:

£8.55 comes from PAYE workers
£1.30 comes from the self-employed
£0.33 comes from farmers

The amount of income tax taken from the PAYE sector has risen steeply over recent years. In 1979, total income tax from the PAYE sector amounted to £648 million. By 1984, the PAYE tax take had risen to £1678 million. Taking inflation into account, this is in fact a **real increase** in the tax take of 60%.

Derek Speirs (Report)

ALRIGHT, LET'S SEE WHO GETS BREAD TODAY YOU OR THE TAXMAN!!

How does the Income Tax System Work?

Everyone who is subject to income tax is allocated a tax free allowance (TFA). This is made up of a personal allowance and a number of additional allowances. Personal allowances vary according to the circumstances:

Single person	£2000
Widowed person	£2500
Married couple (opting for joint assessment)	£4000
Deserted, separated, unmarried parent	£4000

An additional £700 allowance is available to those on the PAYE system, rising to £1400 for a married couple. There is also a series of special allowances for a disabled child (£600), for a dependant who is blind (£600), for a disabled spouse (maximum of £2500) and for those over sixty-five years (£200). Personal allowances and special allowances are added together to work out how much you can earn **tax free**. A single person on the PAYE system can earn £2700 tax free, and more if she or he is entitled to special allowances.

Tax Rates

Once your tax-free allowances are deducted from your gross income, the remainder is subject to tax at different rates. The higher your **taxable** income, the higher the rate of tax you pay.

The standard rate of tax is 35%, the other rates are 48% and 58%. Taxable income up to £4700 is taxed at 35% for a single person, on table A. You are allocated to a tax table depending on the size of your taxable income (i.e. the income you earn **above** the amount you may earn tax-free, £2700 for a single person with no special allowances).

Taxable Income		Rate of Tax
Single Person		
Table A	First £4700	35%
	Next £2800	48%
	Rest	58%
Table B	First £6227	48%
	Rest	58%
Table C	All	58%
Married Couple (opting for joint taxation)		
Table A	First £9400	35%
	Next £5600	48%
	Rest	58%
Table B	First £12,454	48%
	Rest	58%
Table C	All	58%

Tax Relief

Tax relief can be claimed on certain personal expenses. Tax relief means that the amount of the allowable expenses is added to your other tax free allowances so the amount of money you can earn before you start to pay tax goes up. For example, those paying Voluntary Health Insurance (VHI) or a mortgage get tax relief, and the self-employed can deduct business expenses against tax liability.

Generally, you get tax relief at the rate you pay tax. Thus someone on a 35% tax rate saves 35p in the £1 on VHI payments. Someone on a 58% tax rate saves 58p in the £1. Life assurance, health insurance and mortgage payments are the most common areas of tax relief. For anyone paying a mortgage, tax relief is considerable:

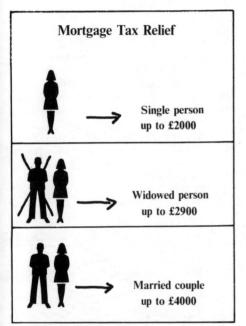

Mortgage Tax Relief

Single person
up to £2000

Widowed person
up to £2900

Married couple
up to £4000

More Deductions

In addition to paying income tax, PAYE workers also pay social insurance. The Pay Related Social Insurance (PRSI) system works as a **further tax on income,** though officially it is not regarded as a tax. It is an earnings-related scheme: the more you earn the more you pay. For most workers, PRSI means a further deduction of about 8% from their wage or salary, but workers in the public service pay a lower rate. On top of this, there is a 1% Youth Employment Levy. So even those on the lowest tax rate (35%) lose on average around 40% of taxable income. On a wage of £140 per week (depending on allowances), you will take home around £100; on £100 a week take-home pay will be about £70.

The Self-Employed

Those who are taxed under schedule D, the self-employed system, submit their own tax returns. Unlike PAYE workers, who are taxed in the current year of earnings, the self-employed are assessed for tax on the **previous** year's earnings. Tax is paid on the profits of the preceding year's business. Tax allowances are calculated on the same basis as is explained above, with the difference that business expenses can be offset against tax liability. These include the following:

— Repair to premises
— Bad/doubtful debts
— Travelling/hotel expenses
— Advertising
— Interest payments
— Other business expenses
— Portion of car expenses
— Portion of rent if residence is used for business & residential purposes
— Portion of phone, electricity expenses

The self-employed assess their own tax liability. There is no deduction at source. Accountants and tax experts find ways to minimise the tax liabilities of the self-employed and of business in general.

Expenditure Taxation

Ireland has the highest rate of expenditure taxation of all the countries in the EEC. Expenditure taxes make up about 40% of all tax revenue. The most important of these taxes are Value Added Tax (VAT) and customs and excise duties.

While a wide range of goods and services is subject to these taxes, by far the heaviest taxes are imposed on just three products: alcohol, tobacco and petrol. Most of what we pay for these products is tax:

74% of the price of a packet of cigarettes is tax
71% of the price of a bottle of spirits is tax
61% of the price of a litre of petrol is tax.

Cigarettes are the most heavily taxed product in the country. The current shop price

is £1.73 for a packet of twenty. Of this shop price, a total of £1.29 is tax. Only 29p is manufacturing cost and 14p is the retail margin.

The VAT system was brought in after Ireland joined the EEC in 1973 as part of the process of harmonising economic conditions across EEC member states. However, the **rates** of VAT have never been harmonised, and Irish rates are particularly high. VAT applies only at the point of **final sale** of a product or service. Any materials or supplies bought for 'further processing' are exempt, so industries can claim refunds for VAT paid in such circumstances. The VAT system is based on 'self-assessment' by retailers who make annual VAT returns. This tends to be time-consuming and tedious to carry out, particularly for a small business without a computerised accounting system.

There are three rates of VAT which apply to different categories of products and services. These rates are 25%, 10% and zero. The top rate of 25% applies to radios, tapes, toys, bicycles, household goods and many other items. The 10% rate covers many different goods from adult clothing and footwear to newspapers and most fuels. It also covers many services such as car repairs, hotel bookings, house purchase and fast foods. Zero-rating applies to many foods and live performances (such as theatre performances and concerts).

The Elusive Wealth Taxes

Wealth taxation is virtually non-existent in this country. Various governments have made pathetic attempts to bring it in. A whole series of wealth taxes has come and gone in the last decade. The property lobby is small but powerful. Death and estate duties were **abolished** in the early 1970s. The coalition government in 1973-77 introduced a wealth tax in their place. It lasted as long as the government, which lost heavily in the 1977 elections. Big farmers deserted Fine Gael on the issue of wealth tax. In 1979, George Colley brought in land tax. It brought in £12 million and lasted less than a year.

A resource tax was brought in in 1980. It managed to bring in £700,000. The target was £7 million every year. It was abolished by the new coalition in 1981.

Since then there has been a property tax, which is being challenged in the courts and has

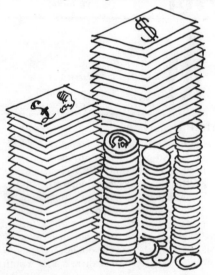

brought in very little revenue. In this year's budget, the coalition deferred the promised land tax once more. They still have not managed to assess the land for tax purposes. In this year's budget, inheritance taxation was abolished between spouses, so wealth can be passed within families virtually untaxed.

Farmers pay little tax. Many thousands of small farmers do not earn enough to enter the tax net, but larger farmers do. Farmers pay about £30 million in tax or about 3.3% of total farm income. 30,000 farmers' tax returns have not been processed because of an industrial dispute in the Revenue Commissioners.

Massive protests by PAYE workers have gained few concessions. The political parties pay more attention to the wealthy sectors of the economy than to those living in real need and who, ironically, finance the bulk of government expenditure.

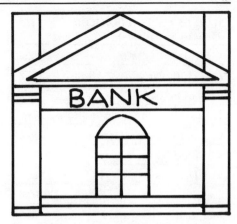

Money Spinners

Despite the severity of the economic crisis in the twenty-six counties, certain sections of this society are extremely wealthy. It is virtually impossible to say accurately where the wealth is concentrated. There is no freedom of information act in this country. Information is scant and unsatisfactory, but profits made by publicly quoted companies and registers of property ownership give some indication of the amount of money made and held in too few hands.

The vast majority of people in this country own **no** personal wealth, other than perhaps the home they live in and their immediate possessions. They own **no** company shares, **no** property to speak of and **no** large bank accounts. They are likely to be mortgaged, in debt and just managing to stretch a shrinking take-home pay packet or welfare payment to meet basic needs.

Inequality and exploitation are everywhere in this society. What is often so difficult to stomach is the continuous moralising from well-paid politcans and employers against the strikers, the welfare 'spongers' and the 'criminal' youth. Politicians' pay, pensions and expenses place them in the well off section of this society, but without shame, they announce cutbacks in health and educational services, miserly increases in welfare rates and refuse to consider pay claims from public sector workers.

Top of the League

The top ten Irish owned companies in the twenty-six counties made £253 million in profits during 1985 alone. **Allied Irish Banks** topped the profit league making £84 million in profits during 1985. The **Bank of Ireland** came a close second with £52.7 million profits. These two banks are also the companies **with the highest market value.** The value of AIB is £373.8 million and of the Bank of Ireland is £343.4 million.

MARKET CAPITALISATION
(Ordinary shares only)

	£m
Allied Irish Banks	373.8
Bank of Ireland	343.4
Jefferson Smurfit Group	278.9
Cement-Roadstone Holdings	239.4
Waterford Glass	172.3
Irish Distillers	126.4
Carroll Industries	109.4
Independent Newspapers	44.9
Aran Energy	44.8
James Crean	40.8

TOP PROFIT EARNERS
(Profits before tax)

	£m
Allied Irish Banks	84.0
Bank of Ireland	52.7
Jefferson Smurfit Group	51.0
Cement-Roadstone Holdings	20.1
Waterford Glass	14.6
Carroll Industries	12.7
Irish Distillers	7.6
Lyons Irish Holdings	3.7
Rohan Group	3.3
Clondalkin Mills Group	3.1

The largest employer and the company which employs the greatest amount of capital is the **Jefferson Smurfit Group.** Smurfits comes third on the profit and market value leagues as well. The same companies appear time and time again on the various top ten tables. The banks, Smurfits, Cement-Roadstone, Waterford Glass, Irish Distillers, Independent Newspapers, Carroll Industries — these are the major Irish owned money-spinners in the companies league in the twenty-six counties.

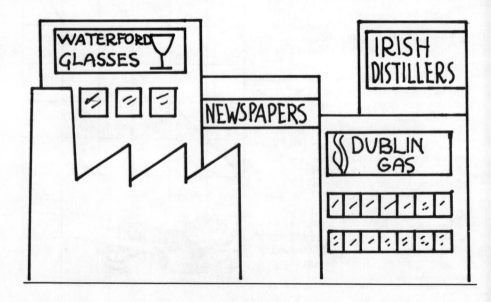

LARGEST EMPLOYERS
(Includes any subsidiaries overseas)

	Employees
Jefferson Smurfit Group	12,000
Allied Irish Banks	8,860
Bank of Ireland	8,608
Cement-Roadstone Holdings	6,935
Waterford Glass	6,400
McInerney Properties	2,400
Irish Distillers	1,560
Independent Newspapers	1,440
Sunbeam Wolsey	1,326
Dublin Gas	1,250

LARGEST CAPITAL EMPLOYED
(Industrial companies only)

	£m
Jefferson Smurfit Group	426
Cement-Roadstone Holdings	342
Waterford Glass	138
Irish Distillers	125
Carroll Industries	57
Dublin Gas	50
R & H Hall	45
Rohan Group	37
Abbey	31
Independent Newspapers	28

While the top companies are raking in the profits, at the other end of the spectrum companies are going to the wall. **More than 3000 companies have collapsed in the last three years.** Between 1983 and 1985, 1437 companies were liquidated and 432 went into receivership. Others were simply wound up.

Surviving the recession has proved impossible for many. Ironically, profits of those at the top of the league have been booming. Smurfits' profits **doubled** from £25 million in 1984 to £51 million in 1985. Cement-Roadstone **doubled** their profits too, from £9 million to £20 million. It's not exactly tough at the top.

The Catholic Church

The catholic church controls enormous wealth in the twenty-six counties, mainly in the form of land and property. The church owns schools, churches, houses and community centres in every county. The assets of the catholic church in the Dublin region are well over £100 million. The Dublin diocese functions as a kind of mini-state, divided into 186 parishes with 234 chapels and churches, 713 schools, 473 houses, and about 100 community centres. There are 700 priests, 750 nuns, and 600 lay staff employed in the Dublin diocese alone.

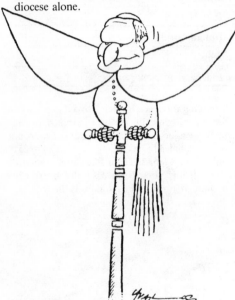

The catholic church is **enormously wealthy.** Its control of property gives it **direct control** over education and community facilities. This control is used to maintain ideological and material power.

Archbishop MacNamara, the present archbishop of Dublin, inherited a highly centralised, hierarchical and powerful organisation. The property empire of the catholic church has been built up on the basis of contributions from a population who can scarcely afford it.

All catholic church property in the Dublin region is owned by the **Saint Lawrence**

O'Toole Diocesan Trust Limited. The trust was set up in 1966 under Archbishop McQuaid. Before that, parish land was owned jointly by the local parish priest, the archbishop and usually one other person. Archbishop McQuaid, and after him Archbishop Ryan centralised all diocesan land. The archbishop chairs the company board and can hire or fire any of the other directors. The directors are all bishops except for Monsignor Williams.

The Trust is extremely powerful. It owns all the property and carries out all investments. Between 1972 and 1984, Archbishop Ryan supervised a major extension of the trust's holdings. In those twelve years, sixty-six parishes were established and fifty catholic schools were opened.

The investments of the trust are shrouded in secrecy. £500,000 is earned from investments every year. No details are made available. Dublin diocesan property stretches to at least 1000 acres. The value of this property empire is extremely difficult to estimate: '£100 million is a conservative estimate of the total property value. It is probably much more.' (**Magill** magazine September 1982.)

Legalised Corruption: The Politicians

'The pay, pensions, expenses and perks which the politicians have assigned themselves are gross.' (Gene Kerrigan, **Magill** magazine October 1985.)

The salaries of the thirty ministers who make up the government amount to more than one million pounds every year. The salaries of all Dáil politicans are nearly 3.5 million. In 1985, Garret Fitzgerald received £47,881 while preaching 'economic restraint' to the rest of us. The average wage of those working in manufacturing industry was £8652. A person on unemployment assistance got £1665. An agricultural labourer got £5081. The average TD got £17,726 in 1985. One-third of this was tax-free.

Gene Kerrigan made a devastating attack on TDs' incomes and pensions in an article in **Magill** in October 1985. He argued that the real value of a TD's salary, taking special tax concessions into account is £21,886. He also pointed out that an average Dublin TD gets £19 a day 'attendance money'. This is worth a further £1653 in a typical year. 'This little bonus is just £2 less than the amount those on unemployment assistance got to live on this year.' (**Magill** October 1985.) Many politicans have their own businesses or professions.

The cost of state cars for the sixteen cabinet ministers came to £840,000 in 1985. Each car costs the taxpayer about £56,000 each year to keep on the road. Ministers of State get cash travel expenses instead of cars.

The greatest scandal surrounding politicians' income concerns their pensions. **Each TD gets a pension of £3595 for life after eight years in the Dáil.** This is paid regardless of age, other jobs or income. A TD with twenty years service gets a life pension of £8989 every year.

References

Association of Combined Residents Associations: Various documents/leaflets on Ground Rent. Unpublished.

Attic Press: Irish Women's Guidebook and Diary.

Budget 1986: Government Publications. February 1986.

Building on Reality 1985-87: Government Publications Office. 1985.

Business and Finance: 'Guide to Taxation' 1986/87. March 1986.

Mary E. Daly: 'The Hidden Workers'. Employment Equality Agency 1985.

Department of Labour: Various brochures on Temporary Employment Schemes.

Irish Congress of Trade Unions: Report to Women's Conference. February 1986.

Irish Congress of Trades Unions: Women at Work ICTU Womens Committee. October 1985.

Irish Times: 'Budget 1986'. January 30 1986.

Irish Times: Public Companies 1985 by John Stanley. December 31 1985.

Irish Times: '1986 Public Service Estimates'. December 19 1985.

Irish Times: 'Profit outflows gobble up export gains' by Ken O'Brien. May 17 1985.

Pauline Jackson: 'Labour force participation of Women in the Republic of Ireland'. Report to Bureau for Womens Equality. Brussels 1985/6.

Pauline Jackson and Ursula Barry: 'Women Workers and the Rationalisation of Services'. Social Studies Spring/Summer 1984.

Magill Magazine: 'The great TD Pension Scandal' by Gene Kerrigan. October 1985.

Magill Magazine: 'The Legacy of Dermot Ryan' by Olivia O'Leary. June 1984.

Magill Magazine: 'The Richest Man in Ireland' by Pat Brennan. September 1982.

Magill Magazine: 'The Farmers and Land Tax' by Olivia O'Leary. October 1984.

John O'Hagan (Ed.): 'The Economy of Ireland' Chapter by Francis Ruane on 'Manufacturing Industry'. Irish Management Institute 1984.

Revenue Commissioners: Report 1983 G.P.O. 1985.

Sunday Tribune: 'Why we each owe £5,714' by Paul Tansey. January 26 1986.

Sunday Tribune: 'The Newest Black Hole' by Paul Tansey. November 24 1985.

Sunday Tribune: 'A Boom Behind Closed Doors' by Paul Tansey. September 30 1984.

Sunday Tribune: 'Dukes Snaps It Up' by Paul Tansey. February 2 1986.

Sunday Tribune: 'Taxes now cost more than food' by Paul Tansey. September 22 1985.

Who Owns Ireland — Who Owns You?: Chapters on Manufacturing Industry and Agriculture. Attic Press. April 1985.

Woman Power: Nos. 1 to 3 by Janet Trewsdale and Mary Trainor. Equal Opportunities Commission for Northern Ireland.

Youth Employment Agency: Annual Report 1985 Brochure: Turning Ideas into Jobs.

Divorce has been a part of the law governing Ireland since the 5th century — the ban on divorce is only fifty years old.

•

A woman's work within the home is not legally viewed as a direct financial contribution, undermining her rights in any sale of the house arising in a separation situation.

•

Between 1980-1983, 8267 applications for barring orders were made to the District Court; 3263 were granted.

•

There were over 3000 applications concerning marital breakdown in 1983 alone.

•

Both the six and the twenty-six counties are legally in a 'state of emergency'.

•

Over 17,000 people have been detained under Section 30 of the Offences against the State Act since 1972. During 1982, only 11% of those detained were charged with any offence.

•

Hundreds of women and men have been imprisoned in the 6 counties under the 'supergrass system' based on the uncorroborated evidence of an accomplice.

•

Only 3% of all crime in the twenty-six counties involves 'offences against the person'. 97% of recorded crime is crime against property.

•

Most of the women in prison in the twenty-six counties are there for shop-lifting, prostitution and drug offences. Half the women in prison are single mothers.

•

Strip-searching of Irish women prisoners in the six counties and England amounts to systematic physical harassment. Martina Anderson and Ella O'Dwyer were strip-searched nearly 500 times between them over a 10 month period.

•

Women have no independent legal status under Irish family law; a married woman's domicile is her husband's; rape cannot legally happen within marriage.

•

The numbers of people in prison has trebled over the last twenty years. Sentences are longer and conditions deteriorate daily.

2
Law and Repression

Repression and the Law

The depth of political and social repression we live under on this island is most clearly illustrated by the legal system. Right wing patriarchal forces have shaped the law on both sides of the border. Both the Constitution and statute law, in the south, take the 'traditional family' as their starting point within a legal framework which dictates a dependent economic and oppressive social position to women. Faced with a growing struggle for legal reform, an alliance of extreme right wing forces have consolidated a powerful political stranglehold over southern Irish society.

The overwhelming defeat of the recent divorce referendum demonstrated the capacity of this alliance to mobilise a mass vote across the country on a pro-family, anti-woman and anti-democratic basis. Their sophisticated campaigning, use of the media and the scale of resources available to them is a frightening reminder of the rigid and reactionary underbelly of Irish society. No political party has been able to unify around a programme of social reform. The catholic church, with its many allies, has been the most powerful social institution to put its full weight against the tide for change in the south. Moral blackmail and political manipulation has been used extensively by the right in their recent campaigns against abortion, contraception and divorce, clearly showing their grip over the media, the political parties and the professions.

Parallel to this climate of social repression, the last fifteen years has seen an extension and consolidation of emergency laws in the north and south of Ireland. The battery of repressive legislation which have denied us our civil rights on both sides of the border owe much to partition. Widespread police and army powers as well as special non-jury courts have become deeply rooted in both legal systems, imposing severe restrictions on the people of this island for over sixty years.

While the struggle for a unified Ireland has focussed attention on the situation of prisoners in the six counties, there has been little coverage of the growing crisis in the prison system in the twenty-six counties. Economic and social conditions in the society outside have spilled over into a prison system which lack the facilities, experience or desire to respond. Average number in prison have trebled over the past two decabes while drug abuse and disease have flourished in conditions of dreadful overcrowding.

Family Law

Family law in the twenty-six counties is riddled with provisions which deny women an independent legal status. It refuses to recognise any unit other than that of the 'traditional family' based on catholic marriage. Over the past twenty years, more and more circumstances have arisen in which women have resorted to the law to protect themselves against violence, to establish maintenance rights and look for separations.

The loss of the divorce amendment is devastating in its consequences for those living in broken marriages. 9,000 women are on welfare categorised as 'deserted wives'; many would have been looking for the means to end their marriages and all the legal complications of their current position. And this is only skimming the surface. What about the tens of thousands of children who are denied their right to a legal relationship with their natural parents? The chaos of the family law situation means that couples who have been separated for years, who may have established new relationships, perhaps involving children, are now condemned to live in a legal limbo.

Within marriage women continue to be viewed essentially as property — without independent domicile, no recognition of marital rape and no recognition of her economic contribution to the home. Family law in the south gives the legal right to a husband to sue his wife's lover in order to get financial compensation for loss of sexual services!

Prospects for family law reform are not good in the wake of the rejection of divorce in the referendum. While the coalition is still promising to reform the domicile and illegitimacy laws and to introduce extended grounds for judicial separation, their position is now extremely weak. It may well be that such fundamental reforms will be put back one more time, leaving the majority of family law essentially as restrictive and oppressive as ever.

Marriage

You may marry at sixteen years with parental permission and at eighteen years without. Any children you have will be 'legitimate' and with rights of succession to any property the two of you may have. This is the 'ideal state' according to both the catholic church and the constitution of the twenty-six counties. The importance of family and marriage is repeatedly highlighted in the constitution which became law in 1937. Despite the fact that the church presents this ideology as one strongly rooted in Irish culture and tradition, experience shows otherwise.

History of Divorce

When the 'free state' was set up in 1922, there was divorce in the twenty-six counties. It was only with de Valera's constitution in 1937 that the prohibition on divorce legislation became part of the law. **The ban on divorce in the republic is only fifty years old.** Extensive historical evidence shows that divorce existed in ancient Ireland under the brehon laws, when mutual consent and adultery were a basis for immediate divorce and the right to

remarry. **Divorce and remarriage in Irish society can be traced back to the fifth century.**

Under British rule, divorce was a part of the law governing Ireland since the time of Henry VIII. After the Act of Union was passed in 1800, Irish couples seeking divorce had to petition the house of lords at Westminster. From 1870 onwards a legal separation from the high court had to be secured before a divorce petition could be granted. It was a long-drawn-out process, so the number of divorces was very low. When the free state was set up in 1922, the senate became the equivalent of the house of lords and it was to this upper house of the Oireachtas (parliament) that applications for private bills of divorce were sent.

Right-wing forces led by the catholic church quickly mobilised against divorce in the 'free' state. In February 1925, the head of the government, W. T. Cosgrave, put a motion to the Dáil to prohibit any further divorce bills coming before the senate. It was passed. However, the senate **refused** to pass the Dáil resolution after a famous debate during which the poet WB Yeats spoke out strongly for minority rights. In theory, Irish citizens could petition the senate to pass private bills granting them divorce, but the climate of hostility and fear surrounding the question of divorce militated against such petitions. This situation continued until the de Valera constitution in 1937, whose clause prohibiting divorce legislation left an intense bitterness, particularly among those of minority religions, and disaffected catholics.

Married Women's Rights

While the laws and social welfare regulations can certainly make life difficult for women outside marriage, they rarely come down on the side of the married woman either.

In law, a woman does not have to take a man's second name on marriage, though in practice their children are usually called by the father's name.

A man may confer his Irish citizenship upon marriage to a non-Irish woman, but an Irish woman cannot automatically do the same for her husband. There is a bill before the Dáil to change this, but it insists that a marriage lasts at least three years and is still intact before the 'alien' partner can apply for citizenship.

Upon marriage a woman takes on the 'domicile' of her husband. Domicile is a legal term which normally refers to the country where you live all or most of the time. Once you are married, your legal domicile is the same as your husband's, whether your marriage has broken up or not, even if he went to China decades ago. Here again, the government has produced a bill to give married women their own independent domicile, but it is not yet a part of the law.

Under Irish law, a husband cannot be accused of raping his wife. When the Criminal Law (Rape) Act 1981 was passed, marital rape was excluded. The Fianna Fáil minister for justice, Sean Doherty, explained this omission by pointing out the 'risks of false allegations'. He also pointed out that if your husband beats you as well as rapes you, it is possible for him to be charged with assault! Research on rape has shown time and again that most rape cases involve a person the woman knows, and often knows well. In this context, or any other, the exclusion of rape inside marriage makes no sense.

Laws passed over the years have allowed women some rights within marriage.

The Married Women's Status Act 1957 allows women the right to sue in their own name (and be sued) and the right, to obtain, keep and get rid of property in their·own name.

The 1965 Succession Act means that where a husband dies without leaving a will, his widow is entitled to the whole estate, or two-thirds if there are children. If he leaves a will, she is entitled to half the estate, or one-third if there are children.

This Act and the Family Law Acts (Maintenance of Spouses and Children 1976 and Protection of Spouses and Children 1981) were brought in at a time when the number of cases of marital breakdown coming before the courts was rapidly increasing. They both refer to spouses, ie either husband or wife, but were mainly designed to give women legal access to property and income within a marriage. One section of the 1976 Act allows a person to sue for maintenance even where they are still living under the same roof as their spouse. This Act is mainly concerned with financial maintenance but also encompasses 'barring orders' where violence is involved. The 1981

Act extended the time limit of barring orders to twelve months and provides for the court decision to be automatically passed to the police for enforcement. However, in many parts of Dublin the police say they have neither the numbers nor the time (nor probably the inclination) to follow up the many barring orders they are in theory responsible for enforcing. While the police have powers of arrest if the 'barred spouse' breaks the court order, they are notoriously reluctant to intervene in 'domestic disputes'. This situation is not, of course, unique to Ireland.

The Family Home Protection Act 1976 prevents either spouse disposing of the family home without the written consent of the other partner. This **does not mean** that married women have automatic joint ownership, nor does it mean that if the house is sold you are automatically entitled to **any** of the proceeds, let alone half. As the law stands at present, you are legally entitled to some of the proceeds if you have made a **direct financial** contribution. This 'direct financial contribution' does not include work in the home, rearing children or feeding and cleaning up after everyone else. You would either have to have been in paid employment or to have inherited money or property to be considered to have made a 'direct financial contribution'. For this reason it is advisable for women to insist that the family home is bought in joint names in the first place.

Single Mothers

Single mothers are usually the sole legal guardians of their child or children. The natural father may be registered on the birth certificate but this does not make him the legal father. It is not legal proof of paternity, although it does help if the mother wishes to sue for maintenance. The mother does not have to consult the father about her child's education and upbringing, even if he is paying maintenance.

A single mother can get an affiliation order through the courts, but this does not constitute legal paternity. She must start affiliation proceedings **before the child is three years old.** Once this is done, she may then sue for maintenance in the normal way. However, maintenance will only be given for the child, not the mother. Solicitors often advise against court proceedings that can be a harrowing experience for the mother. She will be cross-examined, and, as in the case of rape victims, all manner of 'dirt' will be used against her if the case is contested. Most single mothers don't put themselves through all the hassle — it's just not worth it.

The child of a single mother is 'illegitimate'. An affiliation order does not 'legitimise' the child. The child of a single mother may inherit her estate (if any) but any 'legitimate' children take precedence. The child can only inherit from maternal relatives or the father and his relatives if specifically mentioned in their wills. Even then 'legitimate' children take precedence, and may challenge it. You can 'legitimise' your child if you marry the father or by getting the man you may marry to adopt your child. Adoption procedures are the same as for everyone else. Or, you can wait for the promised legislation to abolish 'illegitimacy'.

Separation and Annulment

In the aftermath of the defeated divorce referendum, the Coalition government has promised to proceed with plans to extend the grounds for judicial separation to include desertion, and constructive desertion, and to establish family courts and mediation services. No timescale has been announced. The fragile state of the coalition after the referendum debacle and their lack of a Dail majority leave the situation very uncertain. In the meantime the situation is as follows:

Foreign Divorce: A man or a couple may establish domicile in another country and obtain a divorce there, according to the laws of that country. This divorce is usually recognised by the Irish courts. Because Irish law says that a married woman has no independent domicile a woman cannot have her foreign divorce recognised if her husband is still living here. Once a foreign divorce is recognised, both parties are free to remarry. (The catholic church does not recognise such divorces and will not remarry either person.)

State Annulment: The grounds for this are so limited that from 1980 to 1983 **only ninety-one applications were made.** Thirty decrees were actually granted. It is very expensive. If an annulment is granted by the state it means that no civil marriage ever existed, so both parties are free to remarry under civil law. But children of the original marriage become 'illegitimate' once civil nullity is granted. (The catholic church does not recognise civil annulment so will not remarry either person).

Judicial Separation — 'Divorce' *a mensa et thoro* (away from bed and table): A petition for a judicial separation can be brought to the high court, if you can afford it. The high court can grant an order for separation on the grounds of adultery, cruelty or 'unnatural

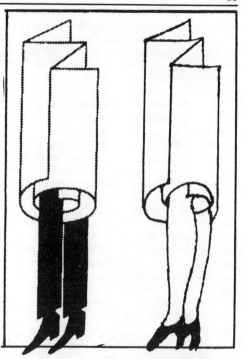

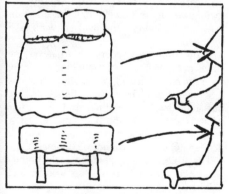

practices! One party is deemed 'at fault' and the other party must 'prove' adultery or cruelty, which are the usual grounds for such an order. There is no right to remarry. The majority of petitions are refused.

Legal Separation: This involves a married couple drawing up a separation agreement which they both sign. It is a legal document agreeing to live apart and making arrangements concerning child custody, property, maintenance, access to children etc. The courts can enforce this agreement. There is no right to remarry. It depends on the co-operation of both husband and wife but is cheaper and easier than a judicial separation.

Barring Orders: A spouse may apply to the district court or the circuit court to bar the other spouse from the family home, in the event of violence. The violent spouse, almost always the husband, can be barred for up to twelve months in the district court. At circuit court level the order can be unlimited. A limited award for maintenance can be made at the same time. This is the most often used legal mechanism where no co-operation exists between husband and wife and where the marriage has broken down. The barring order will only be granted in cases of provable physical violence. Due to the clogging up of the courts with cases there can be delays of up to a year. In 1983 the district court received 1697 applications for barring orders. 848 were granted. In the same year, the circuit court received 242 applications. 129 were granted. Between 1980 and 1983, total applications to the district court were 8267. 3263 were granted.

Church Annulment: In two words — lengthy and expensive. Even when the catholic church does annul a marriage, it may lay blame on one partner and refuse that person permission to remarry. Annulment can be had from the catholic church where the marriage has not been consummated (no sexual intercourse has taken place), the marriage took place under duress and in certain other circumstances. Both partners must submit to lengthy interrogation on the most intimate questions to a panel of clergy and others. The state does not recognise church annulments. After a full annulment, the catholic church will marry you again, but under the state law, this is bigamy. During 1980-83 2849 petitions for annulments were made to the catholic church. Only 326 were granted.

Desertion: There are over 9000 women in receipt of deserted wives' allowance or benefit. However, if you are under forty years of age and have no children, you are not eligible for these payments. It is administered by the Department of Social Welfare. It is means-tested, so any wage a woman may earn or any maintenance she may be receiving could disqualify her. Living with a man could also disqualify her. There is no allowance for men. There is no right to remarry.

Cohabitation: Living with a man outside marriage is not recognised by the law. The welfare system may cut allowances or benefits to a woman living with a man (and they frequently do) even though no legal relationship exists. Children of this relationship are illegitimate.

If a woman and a man live together after a marriage has broken down for one of them, the situation is worse. If the woman was never married but the man is separated, then any children they have are illegitimate. They have no inheritance rights. They may be specifically mentioned in his will, but once again 'legitimate' children (and his legal wife) take precedence.

If the women is separated, whatever the status of the man, then any children they may have are considered to be the children of her first marriage. Their legal father is her husband, despite separation and no matter what is put on the birth certificate. Their natural father cannot adopt them because 'legitimate' children cannot be adopted.

The protection, albeit limited, of the Family Law Act, does not extend to women and children living with a man she is not married to. A legal separation agreement between two people who have not been married has no status. He can sell the family home you share without your permission. You cannot get a barring order. You cannot claim maintenance for yourself or your children. Legal partners take precedence in inheritance. If your partner dies, you will not be entitled to a widow's pension: you will have to wait until your legal husband dies (if you have one).

While the law refuses to recognise the reality of such relationships, the welfare system certainly does: though you cannot claim deserted wives' benefit or allowance if the man leaves, your unmarried mother's allowance will be cut off if he is discovered, even though you are legally a single mother, with illegitimate children, and with no legal relationship to him. This is the case **whether** the man is supporting you or not.

Scale of Marital Breakdown

There are no 'official' statistics on the level of marital breakdown in the twenty-six counties. The 1986 census of population is the first that will allow marital status to be defined as anything other than single, married or widowed. Legal separations, foreign divorces, desertion and judicial separations will be recorded. The accuracy of such information will be difficult to assess for some time to come.

The Divorce Action Group estimates that over 70,000 people, including children, are affected by marital breakdown. Looking at the figures for the numbers going through the courts, initiating annulment proceedings and applying for deserted wives' payments in one year, the scale of marital breakdown is obviously extensive. In 1983 alone there were:

33	applicants for state annulments
8	applicants for judicial separation
631	applicants for catholic church annulments
1939	applicants for barring orders
655	new deserted wives' allowance

There are no figures available for the number of foreign divorces, legal separations, people simply moving out or applicants for deserted wives' payments which were rejected. **Yet, there were over 3000 applications concerning marital breakdown in just one year.**

The Divorce Referendum

The result of the divorce referendum is a major set-back for the women's movement and the progressive forces in this society. It is a body-blow to the tens of thousands of women, men and children whose hopes rested on the reform of family law. The pattern of voting was almost an exact replica of that in the 1983 anti-abortion referendum, confirming the existence of a conscious right wing alliance against social reform, particularly opposed to any attempts by women to assert greater control over our lives.

As it stood, the terms of the constitutional amendment were highly restrictive. Getting a divorce would have involved extensive legal procedures and a long waiting period. Its defeat means that the constitutional prohibition on the introduction of divorce legislation remains intact.

The amendment was defeated in a poll in which 63% (1,474, 123 people) voted. Nearly two out of every three voters rejected divorce; 63% voted NO and 36% voted YES. Just three years ago, 66% voted in favour of the anti-abortion amendment and 33% voted against. History **does** repeat itself.

The Campaign

Just days after the Coalition government outlined their terms for divorce, opinion polls showed six out of ten people in favour of the change. Eight weeks later, one in four had **changed** their minds. Nearly one million people voted NO, **six out of ten rejected divorce.** This incredible turnaround represents the most dramatic shift in public opinion during a campaign, this country has ever seen.

If the referendum was lost on any one issue, it was probably lost on the issue of land and property. The emotive issue of subdividing the land and small businesses was latched onto by the anti-divorce forces in a highly effective way, ensuring the defeat of the amendment in rural areas in particular. But the anti-divorce campaign also targeted women, holding up the spectre of impoverished women rearing children single handedly, with little state support. What was so unpalatable about this tactic is that it is precisely this situation that so many women are **actually in at the moment.** The right cynically exploited the economic dependence of women, a position actively supported by their own ideology, to spread fear among women in both urban and rural areas.

It should also be highlighted, that the publication by the government of 'outline proposals' for divorce legislation left the ground wide open for the anti-divorce campaign. No detailed refutation of the points they raised on property, pensions and welfare could be made by the pro-divorce forces, tied as they were to the vague government statements. The Divorce Action Group opted against putting forward its own independent position on welfare and property rights, a decision they are probably already regretting.

The Political Parties

The spectacle of Irish political parties running for cover on questions of social reform has a long history, and this referendum proved no exception. Fine Gael proposed the amendment in theory, but in practice was deeply divided with many of its key figures and members actively campaigning against. From its very first press conference and the announcement that Peter Barry and Michael O'Leary were to run the campaign, it was clearly a non-starter and not taken seriously by those in command. The Labour Party, already decimated electorally, made little impression and also had key members campaigning for the other side.

Fianna Fail announced itself 'neutral' and then proceeded to campaign heavily against divorce, made its political party machine available to the anti-divorce campaign and produced a party political broadcast urging people to VOTE NO. The so-called 'progressive democrats' disappeared from view, playing no role in the divorce campaign except a few leaflets at the odd polling station.

Prospects for the Future

As the dust begins to settle after the referendum, it is worth looking at the likely consequences for existing family legislation. While the domicile bill has still a good chance of becoming law, the issues of property and land which became so critical during the referendum, may yet stymie the illegitimacy bill.

HOW THEY VOTED ON DIVORCE (1986) AND THE ANTI-ABORTION AMENDMENT (1983)

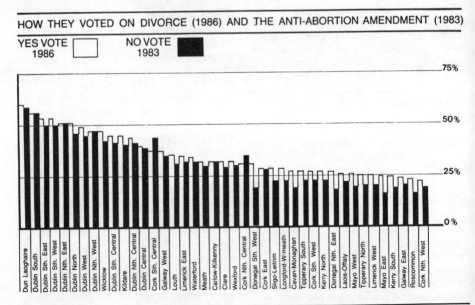

With divorce definitely off the agenda, members of the government parties, Fianna Fail and the anti-divorce campaign have begun to talk of extending the grounds for civil nullity. William Binchy, a major anti-divorce campaigner, is also the researcher of the Law Reform Commission, which has put forward extensive proposals in this area. Grounds for civil nullity could be extended to include, they suggest, cases in which one partner has 'a strong homosexual orientation'; where fraud or duress is involved; cases of non-disclosure of the intent to desert, to avoid having children, of sterility or of non-consummation of the union. Such propositions could form the basis of a ludicrous situation in which marriages could be declared **never to have happened** in a whole series of cases covering sexual orientation and fertility. Children of such non-marriages, even with a reform of the illegitimacy law, would be declared non-marital children. The implications for custody of and access to children by, for example, lesbian mothers or gay fathers are horrific.

This society is heading towards an increasingly polarised and bitter social situation. Disaffection from the state and the political parties is deepening. Demoralisation and depression is spreading fast among those who have put such energy into fighting for social change. However, it is likely to turn to anger and revolt, especially among those who find their personal lives restricted, interfered with and legally confused, under a legal system that lacks both flexibility and compassion.

How the Country Voted
Constituency by Constituency

	Yes	No
Carlow-Kilkenny	31.5%	68.5%
Cavan-Monaghan	27.3%	72.1%
Clare	31.4%	68.1%
Cork East	29.3%	70.2%
Cork Nth Central	30.3%	69.2%
Cork Nth West	20.8%	78.5%
Cork Sth Central	37.4%	62.2%
Cork Sth West	26.8%	69.6%
Donegal Nth East	26.5%	73.0%
Donegal Sth West	30.1%	69.6%
Dublin Central	38.9%	60.5%
Dublin Nth	50.5%	49.2%
Dublin Nth Central	43.8%	55.8%
Dublin Nth East	50.8%	48.8%
Dublin Nth West	47.4%	52.2%
Dublin South	54.2%	45.4%
Dublin Sth Central	45.2%	54.1%
Dublin Sth East	53.4%	46.0%
Dublin Sth West	53.3%	46.0%
Dublin West	48.7%	50.1%
Dun Laoghaire	58.5%	41.0%
Galway East	23.1%	76.3%
Galway West	36.6%	62.5%
Kerry Nth	26.7%	72.5%
Kerry Sth	23.9%	75.5%
Kildare	44.7%	54.7%
Laois-Offaly	26.4%	72.8%
Limerick East	35.0%	64.6%
Limerick West	24.7%	74.6%
Longford-W/meath	29.0%	70.2%
Louth	35.6%	63.7%
Mayo East	24.1%	75.1%
Mayo West	26.1%	73.0%
Meath	31.5%	67.8%
Roscommon	22.5%	76.7%
Sligo-Leitrim	29.2%	69.8%
Tipperary Nth	25.4%	73.9%
Tipperary Sth	27.0%	72.3%
Waterford	32.7%	66.2%
Wexford	30.6%	68.9%
Wicklow	46.8%	52.9%

Total

Dublin	Yes 49.9%	No 49.7%
Rest of Leinster	Yes 34.3%	No 65.0%
Munster	Yes 29.5%	No 63.1%
Connacht	Yes 27.9%	No 71.3%
Ulster	Yes 27.8%	No 71.7%

See page 91 for Map of Ireland *showing breakdown of the Divorce Referendum voting patterns.*

Legal Aid in the Twenty-six Counties

Criminal Legal Aid

Legal aid is available for those charged with criminal offences and deemed eligible under a means test. Generally, if you are on welfare you get it — if not you don't. The legal aid system for criminal cases **only covers court proceedings.** If you want advice in a police station or legal advice in general you are not covered. Access to criminal legal aid only arises once you get to court and the judge makes an order. Once you have been awarded legal aid, you select from a panel of solicitors and barristers. If you can't select one, the court will allocate a solicitor from the panel. Solicitors and barristers get paid according to the number of cases they handle and the time involved. Some make a fortune — up to £100,000 over one year. While office expenses are involved here also, individual gain can be extensive. The criminal legal aid scheme cost about £1.5 million in 1985. The major problems are that often those who need it most don't get awarded legal aid and it does not cover advice, arrest and detention.

Solicitors and Barristers who earned £10,000 or over under the criminal legal aid system during 1984/85
These payments are taxable earnings. They exclude VAT, travelling, subsistence and other payments.

Solicitors	
J. Cantillion	£10,340.52
Fergus Fahy	£14,113.35
J. P. Gaffney	£20,569.78
B. Gunn	£11,897.68
M. E. Hanahoe	£36,452.68
Gordon Hayes	£13,165.49
G. Lambe	£13,265.28
R. Lynam	£26,050.86
T. Lyons	£36,753.34
Pat McCartan	£96,102.42
T. E. O'Donnell	£20,869.63
Garret Sheehan	£77,818.26
Myles Shevlin	£34,960.41
Barristers	
Paul Carney	£25,758.54
Patrick Gageby	£26,617.00
M. Gray	£14,710.50
Adrian Hardiman	£10,667.58
Hugh Hartnett	£16,173.22
Greg Murphy	£32,481.16
Rex Mackey	£13,413.74
Patrick McEntee	£30,365.17
Kevin O'Higgins	£23,826.53
Tom O'Connell	£14,774.79
Seamus Sorohan	£18,243.73
Barry White	£30,694.14

Civil Legal Aid

An extremely inadequate civil legal aid system was introduced in the twenty-six counties following a victory by Josey Airey in the European Court of Human Rights. The court ruled that civil legal aid was a human right. Unfortunately it was a general ruling which did not define the kind of legal aid system which should be made available. This gave the state the loophole it needed. As a result, we have a piecemeal system of civil legal aid, completely overburdened, excluding from its coverage many critical areas of civil law. It is not even free.

Up until the late 1970s, the free legal aid centres (FLAC) run by law students and sympathetic solicitors and barristers provided the only free civil legal aid in the country. The Pringle committee was set up to look into the question in 1974, but nothing was done with its recommendations until Josey Airey won her case. In 1980 the government scheme eventually came into being, after years of denying those who could not afford it the right and the means to take a civil case.

The state set up the cheapest possible service, designed to ensure that it would not create any waves within the legal/judicial system in the twenty-six counties. No panel of solicitors or barristers was used, as is the case under the criminal legal aid scheme. A few law centres were opened with permanent staff: eight full-time and a few part-time. There are three in Dublin, two in Cork and one each in Galway, Sligo and Waterford. The centres provide legal advice and legal aid.

Getting Legal Aid

To get legal aid, you must get a certificate from the civil legal aid board, which is composed of government appointees. It is a highly bureacratic system under which an applicant must satisfy a means test, come within the right category and have a 'reasonable' chance of winning. Emergency certificates can be issued in some situations.

Means Test

Anyone whose disposable income is over £5500 per year is excluded from the civil legal aid system. Disposable income is defined as take-home pay with allowance for rent, dependants, child-care payments, disabilities etc. Even those on welfare can be excluded under this system.

If your 'disposable income' is between £3500 and £5500 per year you must make a 'contribution' depending on the cost of the case. If your 'disposable income' is less than £3500 you pay the minimum: £1 for advice and £15 for a court appearance. **Civil legal aid is free to no one,** though recently a maximum contribution for those on minimum welfare payments of £15 was introduced.

Income (Disposable)	Payment
Up to £3500	£1 or £15
£3500-£5500	Often high payments
Over £5500	No civil legal aid

Excluded Areas of Civil Law

In addition to a very stringent means test, which excludes many from civil legal aid, certain areas of law are excluded altogether. No civil legal aid is available in case of:

— Defamation
— Debt collection
— Consumer cases (for amounts under £150)
— Social welfare appeals
— Employment Appeals Tribunal
— Test cases

Such restrictions governing the civil legal aid scheme are completely unacceptable. Consumer cases, welfare appeals and employment appeals cases are critical areas of civil law, where legal aid is essential. In effect, family law cases are the only cases being covered for civil legal aid and then only for those who get through the means test. In fact, the 1984 civil legal aid board report states that of the cases for legal aid which were deemed eligible that year, 95% were family law cases. Other areas are being excluded. 1300 applicants for civil legal aid were refused in 1984 alone (500 were deemed ineligible under the means test; 150 were deemed outside the scheme: others were criminal cases etc). With the proposed changes in family law such centres will be overrun. Centres already close regularly due to the overload of cases. At one stage recently all three centres were closed in Dublin.

Law centres should exist in every area of urban and rural Ireland. The civil legal aid system is centralised, inaccessible and inadequate. It is completely underfunded. Community legal centres are a basic right, a right this state refuses to fund.

The last of the independently run law centres, Coolock Community Law Centre in Dublin, is in a constant state of crisis. They are currently funded by the Department of Social Welfare. Funding is never guaranteed for the future. 500 cases are handled every year by three full-time staff. Coolock covers consumer cases, welfare appeals and employment appeals, cases not covered by state law centres.

Despite Josey Airey's victory, the state refuses to provide a comprehensive free legal aid system based on community law centres, backed up by panels of solicitors and barristers, giving applicants a choice of representation. Maybe the only course is back to

Crime

Europe on this one.

Crime hysteria has engulfed the country over the last few years. Much of the obsession with crime has been orchestrated by part of the media and particulary by some of the daily newspapers. Little attention has been paid to the fact that the vast majority of recorded crime is extremely petty in nature. Less than 3% of all incidents reported to the police involve any physical damage or hurt to people.

Appalling economic and social conditions force more and more working-class people to risk imprisonment to survive. Getting into debt, going on the 'game', ending up as a drug addict — all of these are serious crimes that can lead to imprisonment. In a society with great inequalities in access to income, wealth and property, criminalisation is another weapon to keep the disadvantaged down.

Despite the impression created in the media, the **crime rate** has actually been **falling** in this country over the past two years, but **fear of crime** has risen at a dramatic rate. It is more than coincidental that the contrived crime hysteria mounted to an all-time peak just at the time when the new Criminal Justice Bill was going through the Dáil. This bill included a whole new array of powers for the police. The wave of crime hysteria has parallelled other waves of reactionary abuse towards travellers, 'unmarried' mothers, dole 'spongers', 'abortionists' and others.

What is Defined as Crime?

The definition of crime changes from society to society. Most of the time, the line between legality and illegality is presented as a natural one, but in fact, it is movable.

'That you will find no professional person in prison for fiddling their tax, no company director for abusing state grants, no property developer for land speculation, no building contractor for using substandard materials says something about the blinkered values of our society.' (Peter McVerry SJ — **Spike Island — The Answer To What?**)

Anti-social activity, such as abusing travellers, paying abysmally low wages or charging exorbitant rents are completely legitimate in this society. Even such illegal activities as tax fiddling or withholding PRSI (Pay Related Social Insurance) payments are ignored: prosecutions and convictions are virtually unknown, and no one goes to prison.

Statistics on Crime

Official crime statistics reflect both the definition and reporting of crime as well as the attitudes of the police force. Even so, official statistics demonstrate the fact that the vast majority of recorded crime is crime against property. Crime statistics are grouped into three categories:

Offences against property without violence: This category includes larceny from cars and shops, receiving stolen goods, fraud and forgery. About 60% of recorded offences come under this heading. This amounted to nearly 60,000 incidents in 1984. The 'detection' rate for that year was 32%.

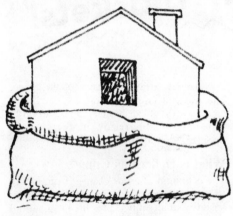

Offences against property with violence: This category does not include violence against people. The violence involved is damage to property, for example, breaking a window to enter a house. It includes burglary, robbery and possession of explosives. There were just over 40,000 such incidents reported in 1984 or 37% of the total recorded crimes for that year. The 'detection' rate was 29%.

Offences against the person: This category includes rape, murder, manslaughter and assault of police. In 1984, less than 3% of recorded incidents came under this heading. Most of those in prison for offences against the person are there for 'assaulting a policeman', a notoriously easy charge to end up in prison for.

Some researchers have attempted to estimate the under-reporting of crime — a risky business at the best of times. A survey carried out by David Rottman and Richard Breen of the Economic and Social Research Institute suggests that incidents reported to the police account for about half to two-thirds of all incidents.

They estimate that between 35,000 and 46,000 burglaries and about 31,000 car thefts take place each year. Over 70% of all burglaries take place in the Dublin area. According to their figures, a house will be entered on average once in twenty-eight years and a car will be stolen from a household on average once in twenty-two years.

Kinds of Crime

The majority of offences against property are of a petty nature. Two-thirds of incidents in 1984 involved losses of less than £200. The vast majority involve no violence of any kind. Of those which do, 86% are burglaries. Breaking and entering is the extent of the violence involved. The following table shows the extent and value of property stolen in 1984.

Value of Property Stolen in 1984				
No. of cases reported in which property was stolen	Value £200	Value £200-£1000	Value £1000-£5000	Value £5000+
81,049	52,486	21,499	6,234	830
	(65%)	(26%)	(8%)	(1%)

The total value of property stolen in 1984 was nearly £34.5 million. The value of property recovered was only just over £2.5 million. Recorded crimes are concentrated in the Dublin area, where about 60% of the total take place. Media hysteria has begun to subside with the passing of the Criminal Justice Act. While the contrived crime panic received hours and pages of media hype, the mounting crisis in the prison system receives much less attention.

The spread of property crime is hardly surprising, given the scale of poverty, unemployment, inequality and drug addiction in this country. It is also connected to the spread of consumer products such as cars and televisions and the increasing proportion of the population concentrated in sprawling urban areas with poor facilities. It can also be seen as an expression of complete rejection of the value system of a society associated with injustice, poverty, repression and exploitation.

Crisis in the Prisons

The severe crisis in the prison system in the twenty-six counties over the past year has been marked by death, disease, riots, protests, hunger strikes and industrial disputes. The build-up of tension goes back over many years.

The preoccupation of the state has been with 'security'. The health and welfare of prisoners has been virtually ignored. Overcrowding and deteriorating health conditions have pushed a number of prisoners over the brink. Four prisoners were found dead in their cells in the space of four months. Drug overdoses, slashed wrists, hunger strikes and the announcement that eight women prisoners and thirty-two male prisoners had AIDS antibodies in their blood have brought the prison crisis to a head.

Despite the scale of the crisis, the Department of Justice refuses to take seriously its responsibility for the health and welfare of prisoners. More and more people going through the prison system have serious drug habits. In 1984, the governor and welfare staff in Mountjoy prison produced a report 'Profile of Mountjoy'. 30% of those in Mountjoy described themselves as drug addicts. The spread of AIDS antibodies among prisoners is directly connected to the use of shared needles within the prison. Regardless of the pervasive drug problem within the prison system, no adequate treatment facilities have been offered. The Prisoners Rights Organisation (PRO) has alleged corruption, stating that drugs have been brought into the prison by prison officers themselves.

The PRO claim that the prisons are operating at 60% over capacity. At precisely the time when over-crowding had become a source of increased tension, Michael Noonan, as minister for justice, announced that early releases were to be severely restricted. The litany of deplorable prison conditions is endless. Hygiene is based on eighteenth-century chamber-pot and slopping-out routines. Education and welfare services are completely inadequate.

The response by the prison authorities to the appearance of AIDS antibodies among prisoners was both inhuman and panic stricken. Prisoners received no proper counselling or advice, were given inaccurate information and were subjected to the terrifying experience of being handled like contaminated objects by prison officers in

gloves and masks, sneering at and abusing prisoners who were isolated from the rest of the prison population.

The prison system here is a 'lock-up', penal one, unlike the systems in other parts of Europe. There is little interest in education, training or rehabilitation. Prisoners in this country are not treated as human beings: prisoners cannot vote; prisoners have no privacy; prisoners have no rights.

The Prison System

There were nearly 2000 people in prison, or other places of detention in July 1985 in the twenty-six counties. Of these, fifty-eight were women. The number of people going through the prison system has increased dramatically over the past two decades. The average number of prisoners on any one day in 1961 was 450, by 1976 it had risen to 1049 and today it is 2000. Not only are greater numbers of people being committed to prison but sentences are longer as well. In northern Ireland there are around 2100 prisoners. 25% are serving life sentences. This compares to a situation in England where just 5% of prisoners are under life sentence. Of the twenty-two member states of the Council of Europe, northern Ireland showed the second highest rate of detention, second only to Turkey, in September 1984.

Who is in Prison?

In the twenty-six counties, about one-third of those in prison are under twenty-one years of age. While the percentage of male youth prisoners has been falling, the number of female youth prisoners has taken a sharp rise. Well over half of those in prison have been there before and about half of these again have been through the prison system on three or more occasions. The prison system acts as a kind of closed system. Once inside the system you are likely to return. An analysis of the prison population for 1983 gives the following breakdown:

Age of those Committed to Prison and St Patrick's Institution in 1983			
Age group	Male	Female	Total
15-21	1389	72	1461
21-25	794	23	817
25-30	643	27	670
30-40	708	32	740
40-50	300	17	317
50+	159	5	164
TOTAL	3993	176	4169

This table shows the number of people committed to prison here over the whole of 1983. It is higher than the earlier figures for the average prison population on any one day.

Women in Prison

The average number of women in prison is way below that of men. In some ways their conditions are even worse. Women are held in Mountjoy or Limerick prison. A growing proportion of women prisoners are under twenty-one years of age, but there are no separate facilities for juveniles, and there is no training unit for women prisoners.

The three main 'crimes' committed by women in prison are shop-lifting, prostitution and drug offences. About half of the women in prison have a history of drug or alcohol addiction. The absence of proper health facilities and treatment is appalling. In addition, education and work facilities are completely inadequate. About half the women in prison are single parents. There are no facilities for children in prison. Visiting conditions are the same for parents as for everyone else.

be planning for a massive increase in the numbers of women prisoners. Where will they come from? From working-class flats and estates across Dublin where dreadful living conditions are the real crime. In prison, women are kept under control with strong tranquillisers like Largactyl, popularly known as the 'chemical straitjacket'.

Strip Searching

'Strip searching is a form of rape.' (Ivor Browne, psychiatrist). Women in prison are always particularly vulnerable. Having a period, being pregnant, getting an infection: these are a nightmare for women prisoners. In the six counties, this vulnerability has become a weapon in the attempts to demoralise and break republican women prisoners. Systematic strip searching has been carried out over the last few years in Armagh Prison and is now happening in Maghaberry, the new women's prison.

Strip searches are carried out by seven or eight wardens (prison officers). Violence is used at any sign of resistance by the women. Women have been held down and literally had their clothes dragged off them, piece by piece during such searches. Strip searching is carried out on women who are sick, menstruating and who have just given birth. Strip searching is physical intimidation and brutality against

Women are imprisoned mainly for economic crimes. Shoplifting cases more often than not involve food and clothing. Women 'on the game' end up behind bars while the men drive off in their fancy cars. The state is building more cells for women. They seem to

women prisoners. Women are strip searched every time they go to court and again on their return. This is designed to demoralise women who are attempting to prepare themselves for critical court hearings.

In Brixton prison in England, Irish women prisoners, Martina Anderson and Ella O'Dwyer, have been subjected to continual strip searching while being held on remand. Over ten months Martina Anderson was strip searched 248 times, Ella O'Dwyer was strip searched 227 times. Martina Anderson was frisked 115 times a month. The only object was to break the morale of these women as they came to trial. Their attempts to get a court order to stop strip searching and end the 'mental stress, discomfort, indignity and inconvenience' failed in London's Old Bailey in May 1986. Ella O'Dwyer in her statement to court said that on one occasion she was strip searched three times within six minutes.

Why are People in Prison?

As highlighted in the last section, the majority of crime concerns property. In the same way, the vast majority of those who go through the prison system are there because they have been convicted of various offences against private property, such as larceny, burglary, malicious damage or trespass. Offences against the person account for a small proportion of prison sentences. The vast majority of these (about 76%) arise from convictions for assault or resisting a garda.

Offences for which Prisoners were Committed in 1983

Offences	Total committed	% of different offences
1. **Offences against the person**	559	100
— Assault/resisting garda	423	76
— Other offences including murder/manslaughter/rape	136	24
2. **Offences against property with violence**	499	100
— Burglary	136	27
— Robbery	147	29
— Malicious damage	193	39
3. **Offences against property without violence**	1808	100
— Larceny	610	34
— Trespass & larceny	512	28
— Trespass with intent	153	8
— Possession/carriage in stolen vehicle	298	16
— Receiving	142	8
4. **Offences not included above**	1303	100
— Road traffic offences including dangerous/drunken driving	653	50
— Forgery & uttering	83	6
— Larceny/possession of Drugs	79	6
TOTAL	4169	

Length of Sentence

The length of time prisoners have been committed to prison for has been rising steadily since 1965. Prisoners are receiving longer and longer sentences.

Year	Sentenced to less than 12 months	Sentenced to 12 months to 2 years
1965	91%	8%
1970	85%	13%
1983	69%	22%

Women prisoners show a particularly marked rise in the length of sentences they are receiving. Only 4% of women prisoners were under sentence of twelve months to two years in 1970. By 1983, 28% of women prisoners were in this category. The overall rise in prison numbers since 1983 reflects the operation of a far more restrictive policy towards the granting of full conditional releases or early releases of 'suitable' short-term offenders. In 1983, 1088 prisoners were released in this way but by 1984, this figure dropped to 435. This policy was backed up by a 'Statutory Instrument' under which two or more prisoners could be put into a single cell. This change took all legal restrictions off overcrowding. Prisoners can now only get a few weeks off their sentences, on the basis of 'good behaviour'.

The Institutions

The majority of prisoners are held in prisons which were built in the nineteenth century. Mountjoy prison, by far the largest, was opened in 1850 and in July 1985 held 539 male

prisoners and thirty-two women prisoners. Portlaoise prison was built in 1830, with an additional block in 1901. It held 212 male prisoners (mainly 'top security' prisoners) in July 1985. Limerick prison, another Victorian style institution was opened in 1830 and in July 1985 held 128 male and twenty-six female prisoners. Cork prison, the other large prison, was opened in 1972 and held 226 male prisoners in July 1985. The rest of the prisons — Arbour Hill, Spike Island, Shelton Abbey, Loughan House, St Patrick's, Shanganagh Castle and the Training Unit — hold about 750 prisoners between them.

Each prison has its particular features. Portlaoise and Limerick prisons are dominated by their intense security systems. Mountjoy and St Patrick's are old, cold and overcrowded institutions. Cork, Arbour Hill and Spike are all partially refurbished military detention barracks. Most of the prisons are based on single-cell structures, the majority of which average thirteen feet by seven and are

Support the prisoners

Derek Speirs.

around nine to ten feet high with about 700 square inches of window. The overcrowding and inadequate facilities have been the major source of tension within the prison system over the last few years.

VISIT A OIN PRISON you may HELP SAVE HER LIFE

Prison Conditions

Even 'officially' the level of overcrowding in the prison system is acknowledged as severe. Prison accommodation in the twenty-six counties is for 1500 prisoners. Yet the average prison population is 2000. At least 500 more prisoners are jammed into the prisons than the accommodation allows for. Much of this arises from the fact that it is almost exclusively a lock-up system. There is no open prison facility for women prisoners. Even the Whitaker report recognises that many of those in prison should not be there, and that custodial sentences should only be used as a 'last resort'.

Visiting conditions in Portlaoise and Limerick were described in the Whitaker report as 'grim to the point of being inhuman'. No physical contact with visitors is allowed. Sentenced prisoners have only one thirty-minute visit a week. Up to three people are allowed on a visit. A maximum of two outgoing letters are allowed every week. All letters, in and out, are 'censored'. Any comment on prison conditions or related

matters is blackened out.

There is a total of twenty probation and welfare officers. There are only eight part-time medical officers to serve the health needs of 2000 prisoners, although health requirements in prisons are often specialised and extensive. Open centres use visiting doctors. Dental services are available, but require special arrangements. Psychiatric services are provided in sessions of three to twelve hours per week in a few of the prisons. There are more priests than doctors attached to the prison system. Clearly, religious welfare takes priority over health services within the prison.

No immediate medical examination is guaranteed on committal to prison. Those admitted at night often wait until the following day — on Friday nights, this can mean no examination until Monday. This has serious consequences for drug addicts in particular. Heroin addicts are placed on a methadone detoxification programme. Therapy sessions are limited. Tranquillisers and other drugs are freely prescribed to prisoners. In a recent case of a drug overdose, a prisoner used prescribed drugs.

Any prisoner serving over one month is entitled to remission of one quarter of the sentence. 'Misconduct' can mean immediate loss of remission. Prisoners are locked up on average sixteen hours a day. A maximum of two hours recreation and two hours work/education are allowed. Prisoners are locked up from 7 or 8 pm until about 8 am the following day. Prison work is tedious and pay is derisory, ranging from £4 to £20 per week, and is conditional on 'satisfactory conduct'.

Cost of the Prison System

The average cost of each prisoner to the state over one year is £29,000. This does not mean that such monies are spent directly on the prisoners — far from it. The maintenance of buildings and payment of staff and security facilities eat up a vast portion of the finance available within the prison system. While expenditure is being savagely cut in other areas of social and health services, the state is systematically planning and financing the extension of the prison system. For example, there are plans to accommodate 144 prisoners in a new women's prison, despite the fact that the average number of women in prison is only around fifty at present.

£91 million has been spent on buildings and equipment over the past fifteen years. The elaborate security system eats up most of the finance in Portlaoise and Limerick.

The 1985 official estimate for prison expenditure was £49.7 million, of which over £12 million was allocated to capital expenditure. The cost of prison staff is 76% of current expenditure.

Expenditure on Prison System	
Dept. of Justice administration	678,000
Other depts. administration	140,000
1550 **Prison Service** (i.e. staff & admin. costs)	30,397,000
Buildings and equipment	1,410,000
Maintenance	1,330,000
Rental	80,000
Education & training services	1,190,000
Other services (food/ medicine/clothing etc.)	4,295,000
Materials, tools etc.	396,000
Probation & welfare services	670,000
Miscellaneous	3,434,000
Capital expenditure (new/refurbished buildings)	12,130,000
TOTAL	54,740,000

The above table gives a clear indication of the small proportion of prison expenditure which actually goes to education, health, probation and welfare. The vast majority of expenditure is on staff and buildings — nearly £50 million out of a total of £55 million.

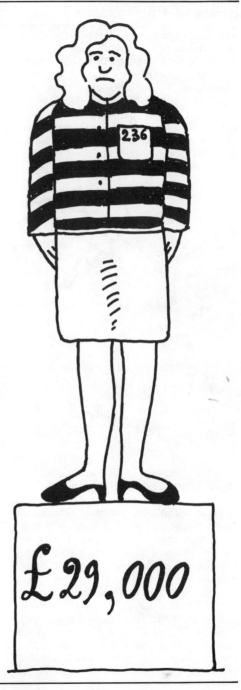

£29,000

States of Emergency

The result of partition on this island has been the creation of two volatile and repressive states. The regular upsurge of political protest over the unification of the country has met a response in the militarisation of these two fragile states. Legislation introduced as an 'emergency' measure has become a permanent part of both legal systems, eroding our civil liberties, affecting criminal law and the media as well as giving enormous powers to security forces on both sides of the border.

Throughout the thirty-two counties of Ireland there are about 50,000 members of the various 'security' forces. In the twenty-six counties the so-called 'unarmed' police in fact contains about 2000 armed men and more recently women. In the six counties there are **three** armed forces, the Royal Ulster Constabulary, the Ulster Defence Regiment and the British Army.

Specialised units responsible for armed surveillance, dawn raids, gathering intelligence and undercover operations are active both north and south of the border. These 'security' forces are equipped with sophisticated technology: computerised files with cross-reference facilities, helicopters, plastic bullets, heavy arms, listening equipment, armoured vehicles and highly specialist communications systems. Cross-border collaboration is at a sophisticated peak. Direct political influence over the legal and judicial system is a characteristic of both states.

In the six counties, whole areas are treated as enemy territory where the population is heavily screened and subject to daily harassment, house raids and mass arrests. Being stopped, searched and questioned is a routine part of moving around and through the six counties. In the twenty-six counties armed units of different specialised squads tear through city streets and working-class areas with the new-found power of plain clothes, unmarked cars and Uzi submachine-guns. We live in a society where civil and democratic rights have been permanently suspended under states of emergency which have become states of normality.

Emergency Law — Thirty-Two Counties

The thirty-two counties of Ireland are officially in a state of emergency. In the six counties, the Special Powers Act of 1922, reinforced by the Emergency Provisions Act 1973 provides the **special legal framework** for the 'state of emergency'. In the twenty-six counties, the Offences Against the State Act 1939, its amendment in 1972 and the Emergency Powers Act of 1976 together form the legal framework for its 'state of emergency'. Under these 'emergency states', special courts without juries, exceptional rules governing evidence and detention without charge are routinely used by the security forces in the whole of Ireland.

Twenty-Six Counties (The Republic)

The Offences Against the State Act was passed in 1939 during World War II. The Act provided for the establishment of a military tribunal under which certain specified offences were tried. At the time most of the cases before the tribunal concerned rationing, particularly petrol rationing. Nevertheless, from the beginning, the Act also covered the activities of 'unlawful organisations' and 'public safety'.

The end of the war did not mean the end of the state of emergency. The **Special Criminal Court** was set up under an amendment to the Offences Against The State Act in 1972. The resurgence of political protest in the six counties was the background to this as well as a whole series of other repressive measures. The 'Progressive Democrat' Dessie O'Malley, formerly minister for justice in a Fianna Fail government, stated at the time that possible 'intimidation of jurors' was the reason for the special court. Many commentators felt that the low rate of convictions in the ordinary courts was actually the critical factor. Instead of the military officers who presided over the earlier tribunal, government-appointed judges presided in the special criminal court. The 'scheduled offences' over which the court was to have jurisdiction included offences under the Explosive Substances, Firearms, Malicious Damages and Offences Against The State Acts.

Special Criminal Court in Practice

Since it was set up in 1972 this non-jury court has been increasingly used for more and more cases involving **non-scheduled offences** such as larceny, forgery and various offences under the Criminal Law and Offences Against the Person Acts.

Nearly 5000 people have come before this court between 1974 and 1984. Of these, 3177 were charged with scheduled offences and 1600 with non-scheduled offences. **This means that one-third of all cases coming before the special court are not those for which the court was set up.** Trial by jury has effectively been abolished for a whole range of criminal charges. In 1974, 62% of those charged in the court were found guilty, by 1977 this dropped to 20%, but by 1983 it was up again to 31%. Sentences handed out by the court have been getting longer every year. In 1976, the average sentence was three years. By 1984, it had **doubled** to six years. These figures do **not** include life sentences for murder. Increased sentences have occurred most frequently in cases under the Larceny and Offences Against the Person Acts, which are non-scheduled offences.

Anyone convicted of a scheduled offence **automatically loses their job** if they work in the public sector. If you are a teacher, busworker, civil servant or street-cleaner you are immediately fired and can never work in government-funded employment again.

There has been very little public debate on the operation of the special criminal court — its use for trying non-scheduled offences has developed with little controversy. Few cases in the special court are reported unless they have earlier received media attention. This lack of debate and coverage is hardly surprising. **The Irish Press, Irish Times** and **Hibernia** have al'

Derek Speirs (Report)

ended up in court as a result of remarks made about the special criminal court.

Judges in the court are appointed by government and are removable **at any time.** This means that **direct political control** is exercised over the court.

Three judges hear each case. Decisions are on a majority basis. **Dissenting judgements are neither given nor recorded.** The court has **absolute power** over its own procedure and can **exclude** any member of the public from its hearings. Amnesty International found that the special criminal court tends consistently to accept police testimony in preference to that of the accused.

The atmosphere in and around the court is tense and intimidating. There is a permanent heavy security presence. The police and army patrol all access points. Anyone attending a case must sign a register. All bags are searched. Top-security prisoners are brought under military escort up and down to Portlaoise prison for court appearances.

Powers of Detention

Non-jury courts were only one of the repressive measures introduced under the amendment to the Offences Against the State Act in 1972. Section 30 gave the police power to arrest and detain people for twenty-four hours, where they suspect that a scheduled offence **has been or is about to be** committed. The detention period can be extended to forty-eight hours simply on the signature of a police superintendent. The 1976 Emergency Provisions Act extended the detention period for seven days — this was in force up until 1978.

'Section 30 is being used as a fishing net to scoop in all those whom the police would like to question, harass or intimidate.' (**Magill** magazine 2 May 1985.)

Over 17,000 people have been detained under section 30 since 1972. Civil liberties are almost totally suspended for anyone detained under section 30. Access to legal advice is regularly denied. Those detained **must** account for their 'movements' over the previous twenty-four hours. Fingerprints, palm prints and photographs are taken, even though charges are rarely preferred. The numbers arrested under section 30 have risen at a dramatic rate over the period 1972-85. In 1972, 229 people were detained under section 30. By 1980 the figure had leapt to 2308 people. The growing use of this repressive measure to 'question', harass, or intimidate is clear from a closer look at the figures. In 1972, 81% of those arrested were charged. Ten years later in 1982, only 11% of those arrested were actually charged.

Only a tiny proportion of those detained are ever actually convicted.

Between 1975-1985: 14,000 people were arrested under Section 30; 500 people were charged; less than 2% of those arrested were convicted under the Act.

The widespread and routine use of repressive powers has meant that thousands of people have been held in appalling conditions in police stations. They have been unable to contact family or friends, denied access to legal advice, and questioned and interrogated on the whim of the police. Many have been taken from home and from work. For some, the consequences have been losing their jobs or missing their welfare for the week. In addition, **2500 search warrants** were issued under the Act in 1983 alone. Prosecutions arose in **only 10%** of the cases in which search warrants were used. The following table shows arrests and charges under section 30 between 1972 and 1984.

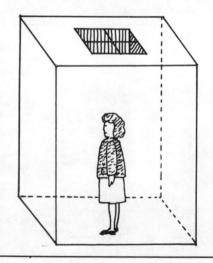

Year	No. of persons arrested	No. charged	% of arrested persons charged
1972	229	186	81%
1973	271	181	66%
1974	602	271	45%
1975	607	116	19%
1976	1015	171	16%
1977	1144	150	13%
1978	912	133	14%
1979	1431	169	11%
1980	1874	168	9%
1981	2303	323	14%
1982	2308	256	11%
1983	2334	363	15%
1984	2216	374	16%

(**Magill** magazine 2 May 1985).

Throughout the mid and late 1970s, allegations were persistently made by those held under section 30 that they had been beaten and forced to sign 'confessions'. Conflicts over such evidence are invariably resolved in favour of the police in the court. In the case of the Sallins mail train robbery case, the Supreme Court found that the accused had suffered injury in police custody but that it must have been inflicted by people other than the police! Amnesty International in a report in mid-1977 concluded that some police were inflicting 'systematic maltreatment' on arrested people. During this period **80% of serious crimes were brought to court on the basis of 'confessions'.**

The routine daily use of emergency powers gives repressive laws an air of normality. The 'state of emergency' in the twenty-six counties affects not just police powers and court procedure; it also affects what we see and what we hear. Section 31 of the Broadcasting Act censors radio and television coverage of particular individuals, organisations and events. Section 31 is not restricted to 'illegal' organisations or individuals who have been convicted of particular offences. No member

of Sinn Féin can be interviewed on radio or television, on any subject, though Sinn Féin is not an illegal organisation (see also the section on the media).

The normalisation of repressive legislation has consequences for the whole area of criminal law. Detention **without charge** has now become part of general criminal law. Emergency provisions have inevitably spilled over into criminal law.

The **Criminal Justice Act 1985** gives general powers of detention for twelve hours (but can go up to twenty hours in particular circumstances). It also introduced majority jury verdicts instead of unanimous verdicts, restrictions on the 'right to silence' as well as increased sentences for a wide range of offences. Despite these general and wide police powers which apply across the board, the abolition of emergency powers has not been considered in the light of such developments. In effect the 'state of emergency' has become a permanent part of the system.

Extradition

Traditionally, extradition for 'political offences' has been refused by the courts in the twenty-six counties. In fact, the Extradition

Derek Speirs (Report)

Act 1965 specifically prohibits extradition for 'political' offences. Persistent and intense pressure from the British government to extradite those they want in connection with the conflict in the six counties has culminated in major changes in the whole area of extradition. Recent court decisions have redefined 'political offences'. Dominick McGlinchey and Seamus Shannon have both been extradited to the six counties in the past year, in the face of open and frequent condemnation by the government in the twenty-six counties of the legal and judicial system in the six counties. Both their cases eventually collapsed in the northern courts because of lack of evidence. Extradition warrants do not have to be backed up with **prima facie** evidence of a case against the accused. In March 1986, the government in the twenty-six counties signed the European Convention on Terrorism which provides for extradition for political offences. This convention has yet to be ratified by the Dáil and is likely to involve legislative changes or possibly even a constitutional amendment.

Six Counties (Northern Ireland)

The six counties have been in a 'state of emergency' since 1922. The Civil Authorities (Special Powers) Act became law when the northern Irish state was set up in 1922. In 1933 it was made permanent. The Special Powers Act gave the Stormont home minister the power to bring in provisions 'for the preservation and maintenance of order'. Under this Act, provisions for internment without trial and exclusion orders were introduced: organisations, meetings, processions and assemblies could be banned and it became an offence to refuse to answer questions. Such regulations were **in addition** to the sweeping powers of arrest and detention which the statute itself conferred on the police. It also established special courts for specific offences. Finally, regulation 22B under the Act provided for the private examination of persons believed to be capable of 'giving material evidence or information'. Such examinations took place in front of a magistrate without any legal assistance. Refusal to answer **any** question was an automatic offence.

Re-organising the Legal System

There was massive opposition, spearheaded by the civil rights movement, to the Special

Powers Act and particularly to internment without trial, which had been introduced under this Act in August 1971. Internees repeatedly alleged that torture, brutality and ill-treatment were a systematic part of the conditions of internment. Six months after internment was introduced, thirteen unarmed civilians were killed when the British army opened fire on a civil rights demonstration in January 1972. This incident came to be known as 'Bloody Sunday'. Soon afterwards Stormont (six counties parliament) collapsed and direct rule from Westminster was imposed. Against this background the British Government was forced to re-organise the legal system in the six counties. The Special Powers Act was eventually repealed, but was replaced by the equally repressive Emergency Provisions Act of 1973. This Act was further consolidated under a Labour government in Britain in 1978. Internment was suspended in 1975 but can be reintroduced at any time. The Emergency Provisions Act only applies to the six counties, not to England, Scotland and Wales. The Prevention of Terrorism Act was introduced in 1976 and applies to both Britain and the six counties.

Army and Police Powers

Under the Emergency Provisions Act, the army and police have the power to detain anyone 'suspected' of an offence for up to four hours 'for the purpose of establishing her or his identity'. There is no 'right to silence'. The police and army also have the **power to search** any premises or place where someone suspected of a scheduled offence is suspected of being **without a warrant**. There is also a provision to seize **and use any property,** a power often used to erect barriers of barbed wire or take over premises.

The police and army have power to **arrest any person without a warrant** who is 'suspected of being a terrorist'. That person can be held for seventy-two hours, and photographs and palm prints may be taken. Suspicion is enough — it does not have to be reasonable suspicion. The vast majority of those detained are never charged. Of those charged the main type of evidence is 'statements' which the accused repeatedly allege were forced out of them under duress.

Under the Prevention of Terrorism Act 1976, there is also a provision to arrest a person 'upon reasonable suspicion of a terrorist offence'. Under this Act, detention is for forty-eight hours but can be extended to seven days by the secretary of state. This Act has been used extensively to detain Irish people travelling to Britain. On average 7% of those detained under the Act are charged. 70% of arrests under this Act are at ports and airports of entry to Britain. This Act has systematically been used to harass the Irish community in Britain, creating a climate of fear and intimidation. Originally this Act was designed for use against the Irish, but more recently it has been used much more widely. Internally to the six counties it is used to allow for an extended (seven-day) detention period.

'The dire conclusion to be drawn from the uses to which emergency powers of arrest and detention are put both in northern Ireland and Britain, is that wherever possible they are applied recklessly, against citizens the overwhelming majority of whom are innocent of any crime'. (Richard Harvey **Diplock and the Assault on Civil Liberties,** Haldane Society of Socialist Lawyers July 1981.)

Proscribed Organisations

The Emergency Powers Act proscribes or declares illegal a number of organisations, membership of which carries a prison term of up to ten years. The Irish Republican Army,

(IRA), the Irish National Liberation Army (INLA) and the Ulster Volunteer Force (UVF) are banned under the Act.

Exclusion Orders

Exclusion orders are carried out under the Prevention of Terrorism Act 1976. Persons can be refused entry to England, the six counties or excluded from anywhere in the United Kingdom. Effectively, the secretary of state can restrict where a citizen lives or moves within the UK or can exclude them altogether under threat of up to five years' imprisonment and an unlimited fine. The person has no right to know the case against her or him. There is no appeal.

Legalised Brutality

The two police interrogation centres which were opened in the six counties in 1977, Gough Barracks and Castlereagh, have been surrounded by controversy. Castlereagh has a particular reputation for brutality and torture, both physical and psychological, which was at its height during the 1977-80 period. Amnesty International produced a report documenting cases of both torture and brutality. The outcry which followed forced the British government to set up an enquiry into interrogation procedures under Judge Bennet. The Bennet report looked only at physical brutality, ignoring the issue of psychological torture completely.

Access to solicitors, family and friends has been constantly denied to detainees and has been the subject of systematic investigation and complaints by the Haldane Society and others. In the six counties, 86% of cases going through the courts in 1979 relied wholly or substantially on 'confessions'. The government of the twenty-six counties took the British government to the European Court of Human Rights alleging brutality and torture. The court judgement held that the British administration had perpetrated **maltreatment** of detainees, not quite defining it as torture.

Diplock Courts

Following the abolition of internment, the non-jury courts were set up under the recommendation of Lord Diplock. The Diplock courts, as they were called, abolished jury trials for scheduled offences under the Emergency Provisions Act. Diplock courts operate under a single judge. This measure, which was to be a temporary emergency measure, is now a permanent part of the legal system in the six counties. The Haldane Society estimates that 80% of cases in the

Diplock courts involve the acceptance of evidence from **members of the security forces** while rejecting that of the accused. There are only sixteen judges eligible to hear scheduled offence cases, so often the **same** judges hear cases **and** appeals.

The 'Supergrass' System

Over the last five years, the regular use of 'informers' has become a key feature of the judicial system in the six counties. Many commentators have associated this new development with the pressure which had built up on the British administration because of the public controversy over brutality during interrogation. The 'supergrass' system involves the use of mainly **uncorroborated evidence of an 'accomplice' in mass trials before a single judge.** Such a system means 'confessions' are not so necessary, as the uncorroborated evidence of an 'informer' forms the basis of the case.

The 'supergrass' trials involve hundreds of witnesses, hundreds of incidents and hundreds of charges. The trials stretch for months with twenty or thirty defendants in the dock. All this incredible detail stretching over such a long period is presented to a solitary judge. One particularly ludicrous aspect of these trials is when the judge **warns himself** of the danger of accepting uncorroborated accomplice evidence, a warning normally given to a jury. Hundreds of people have been convicted under this discredited system. Despite cases in which the 'supergrass' has been described **by the judge** as a 'perjurer' or of 'unsound character' and cases in which evidence was **contradicted by fact,** convictions have been handed out wholesale. The 'supergrass', often facing a lengthy sentence before agreeing to give 'evidence', is promised immunity or a much reduced sentence, money and a new life once her or his evidence is satisfactory. The government of the twenty-six counties has been pushing for a refinement of this system based on three judges rather than one, smaller trials and stricter control over uncorroborated evidence. Some changes are on the cards as one of the 'concessions' associated with the Anglo-Irish agreement.

Effective Internment

The bottleneck in the courts in the six counties means that prisoners are regularly being held on remand for up to two years before coming to trial at all. The length of the 'supergrass' trials and the long wait for an appeal together result in situations in which the accused spend four years or more going through the judicial process.

This is the equivalent of a seven- or eight-year sentence (taking remission into account). At the end of the four years, where an appeal is won, **no compensation** is available to those who have been incarcerated for so long. Bail is rarely granted in the Diplock courts.

Conclusion

The spill-over of 'emergency legislation' into criminal law has taken place in almost parallel fashion in both Britain and Ireland. The Offences Against the State Act ushered in the Criminal Justice Act in the twenty-six counties. The Prevention of Terrorism Act brought the Police Act in its wake in Britain. These developments are not unique to this part of the world. In many parts of Europe, particularly where social and political upheaval has been intense, democratic rights have been undermined. Repressive legislation has spread through the legal systems of many countries and Ireland is ahead of the field.

References

Council for Status of Women: 'Irish Women Speak Out'. Co-Op Books 1981.

Council for the Status of Women: Review June 1985.

Divorce Action Group: 'A Case for Divorce' 1985.

Evening Herald: 'Strip-search Ban Move Fails'. May 1 1986.

Garda Crime Report 1984: Government Publications Office June 1985.

Richard Harvey: 'Diplock and the Assault on Civil Liberties'. Haldane Society of Socialist Lawyers. London July 1981.

Ian Hart Memorial Lectures 1985: 'Institutions — Safety Belts on Strait-Jackets'. Simon Community 1986.

Irish Press: 'How the basis for extradition has changed' by Michael Farrell. February 1986.

Irish Times: 'Politicians Ran Prisons To Suit Themselves' by Sean Flynn. January 27 1986.

Irish Times: 'Official Neglect Met Drug Problem' by Sean Flynn. January 28 1986.

Irish Times: 'Litany of Tragedy in the Prisons' by Sean Flynn January 29 1986.

Irish Times: 'Department Holding Back Prison Reform' by Sean Flynn. January 30 1986.

Magill Magazine: 'A Very Special Court' by Derek Dunne. May 16 1985.

Magill Magazine: 'Crime Hysteria' by Gene Kerrigan and Helen Shaw. April 18 1985.

Magill Magazine: 'Section 30: Arrests soar' by Gene Kerrigan. May 2 1985.

Peter McVerry S.J.: 'Spike Island — The Answer To What'. Resource Publications 1985.

Office of Minister of State for Womens Affairs: 'Agenda for Action'. Government Publications Office 1985.

Office of Minister of State for Womens Affairs: Womens Affairs Review 1985.

Office of Minister of State for Womens Affairs: Women and the Law 1986.

Rape Crisis Centre: Annual Report 1985.

Report of Joint Oireachtas Committee on Marital Breakdown: Government Publications Office 1985.

Ailbhe Smyth: 'Women's Rights in Ireland'. Irish Council for Civil Liberties. Ward River Press 1983.

Sunday Independant: 'Suicide in Our Prisons' by Frank Byrne. January 26 1986.

Whittaker Report: The Irish Prison System. G.P.O. 1985.

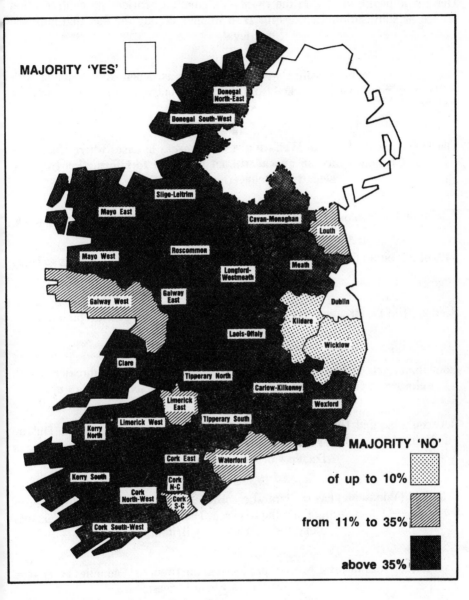

*Pattern of voting in the Divorce Referendum
1986.*

The public health service in the twenty-six counties provides no contraception service or sterilisation facilities for Irish women, despite the fact that both are legal.

•

The welfare system classifies women claimants as dependants. Women with children are continuously blocked from claiming as unemployed under the welfare system.

•

The Department of Social Welfare gives *no reasons* in cases where claims are rejected. Claimants face an appeal without any right to information from the Department concerning its decision.

•

32% of all households in the six counties live on an income of less than £75 a week.

•

54% of ads on RTE portray women as 'decorative'; 24% as home-makers and only 4% as working in the economy.

•

Section 31 of the Broadcasting Authority Act denies elected public representatives access to RTE.

•

Community arts and many theatre groups and arts centres are threatened with closure as funding under temporary employment schemes dries up.

•

Between 1984 and 1985 there was a 50% increase in the smog level in Dublin. Smoke levels rose *above* EEC limits on 124 occasions during 1984/5 according to Dublin Corporation monitoring.

•

Sellafield (Windscale) has the largest recorded source of radioactive discharge in the world — it goes straight into the Irish sea. There are eighteen nuclear reactors along the west coast of Britain.

•

Over 30,000 tons of toxic waste is produced in the twenty-six counties every year — no one knows where it goes.

•

There are about 3,000 people homeless in the twenty-six counties. Only 7% of the beds in shelters and hostels are provided by the State.

3
Social Control

Social Control

Quite different aspects of social life in the twenty-six counties are brought together in these chapters. 'Living on the Edge' looks at the circumstances of those who have paid the price of the economic recession, north and south. The scale of unemployment and dependence on welfare and its effect on different sections of the population is explored. Turning to the environment, the link is made between the natural physical state of both city and countryside and the social conditions of badly planned and serviced housing areas. Too often discussion on the environment is limited to areas of particular scenic beauty while ignoring the living conditions of a growing proportion of the population.

Social and cultural expression is the theme of chapters on the Arts and the Media in the twenty-six counties. From questions of censorship to the problems associated with lack of funding, the explosion in Arts activities is in danger of being forced into a cul de sac. Temporary employment schemes have enabled theatre groups and other projects to survive, but for many this option is fast becoming obsolete. The state controlled media due to the increasing dominance of imported programmes is unable to provide vital resources to home-produced programmes. Every cultural tradition develops through exploring new themes or using different approaches. In an age of high-tech, high powered sophisticated communications, funding to home produced Arts and Media is essential to the survival of cultural expression and its traditions.

Every society develops its own method of **social control.** None relies exclusively on the law. Inside the family, our basic unit of social control, religious, cultural and moral values are transmitted from one generation to the next. In most urbanised societies, wider institutions — such as the education system or the media — have become increasingly important as systems of control.

Political power in the twenty-six counties is highly centralised. Local authorities have little autonomy over their own areas. Politicians feed off a system of political patronage, dispensing favours in return for votes. Decentralisation of power and control is unheard of in the Irish political system.

In the twenty-six counties, it is the catholic church that acts as the dominant social force. This central role of the catholic church does not simply derive from a moral authority, it is

concretely based. The catholic church:

* controls and administers the education system at first and second level
* determines the kind of health facilities available
* shapes much of the social legislation on the statute books.

In recent years, the catholic church has found itself on the defensive. Demands for social reform are breaking through into the political system. Social conditions are changing at such a pace that nineteenth-century legislation is being pushed aside. In the face of this desire for reform, the catholic church has stubbornly maintained the most rigid position on mixed marriages, contraception, divorce and sexuality. In other countries, the catholic church has been forced to accept new and changing social realities, but here it has refused to loosen its grip, and in the process, has spawned a myriad of right-wing, fundamentalist catholic organisations. Family Solidarity, the Responsible Society, the Society for the Protection of the Unborn Child (SPUC) and others are the new face of Irish catholicism.

They have formed alliances with older, better established organisations such as Opus Dei and the Knights of Columbanus. All these organisations share an obsession with and a fear of human sexuality. Opposed to divorce, sterilisation, contraception, abortion, lesbianism and homosexuality, they have adopted political campaigning with a vengeance.

Contraception

The major battle between right-wing catholicism and the movements for social change has been over contraception. It has raged with barely a breathing space for over fifteen years — and is not over yet. The women's liberation movement of the early 1970s forced the contraception issue onto national headlines with the notorious 'contraception train'. Feminists took the Belfast-Dublin train returning with handfuls of contraceptives which they flaunted at customs officials and cameras. Several attempts to bring in contraception legislation failed over the following decade.

Throughout the 1970s, the family planning clinics defied the law, importing and distributing contraceptives. The famous Magee case established the right of married couples, on grounds of marital privacy, to import contraceptives for their own personal use. This loophole in the law allowed the family planning clinics to continue to operate, as long

as they did not actually sell the goods, as sale of contraceptives remained illegal.

Eventually in 1979 a highly restrictive and completely unworkable piece of legislation made contraception legal — for some. You had to have a medical prescription in order to get contraceptives, even non-medical and barrier forms of contraception. The law, though ambiguous, suggested you had to be married in order to be issued with a prescription. In any case, it was virtually impossible for unmarried people, especially in rural areas, with limited access to liberal doctors and pharmacists, to get contraception. Even married people had great difficulty, unless they were lucky enough to have a sympathetic doctor and chemist.

In 1985, the coalition government made an attempt to bring the law into some contact with the lives and sexual practices of Irish people. The sale of contraceptives to people over eighteen was legalised, regardless of

marital status. The main change was that medical prescriptions would now be required only for medical contraceptives.

However, the health service in this country takes **no responsibility** for birth control facilities. There are health centres in every local area in the twenty-six counties, but they do not provide information, advice on contraception, nor any contraceptive devices.

Family planning clinics continue to operate, but their services are restricted to certain urban areas. Mail order is available but this cannot be viewed as adequate, as the clinics themselves would agree. It is the responsibility of doctors to provide both advice and prescriptions. Not all of them do. Few are trained to fit a diaphragm or insert a coil; most simply write prescriptions for the contraceptive pill. By international standards the pill is massively over-prescribed here and, given the health risks attached to its use, this is extremely worrying. Rural women are the victims of particularly inadequate services. They must travel long distances, often in secret, to get to a clinic. Moral pressures from unsympathetic doctors, chemists, neighbours

and the clergy can be intense. We are still in a situation where only a tiny minority of chemists will even stock condoms.

In the face of all this, the western health board, in the twenty-six counties, announced recently that it is 'satisfied' with the current level of family planning service in its area. The board has no intention of improving the service.

Sterilisation

More recently, the catholic church has raised its banner against female sterilisation. For years it has ensured that no hospitals in the twenty-six counties would provide such a service. Growing demand from women pushed some hospitals into making sterilisation available. Then the catholic church put its foot down.

Sterilisation is not illegal in the twenty-six counties. Yet the overwhelming majority of public hospitals do not provide it. It is available through the private clinics, but not for women on the medical card. Strangely, female sterilisation is most difficult to get in Dublin. In 1985, thirty-five operations were carried out in the Rotunda and three in Holles St. The Coombe did none.

In Galway, the Regional hospital averages 100 operations every year. The Victoria hospital in Cork has a twelve-month waiting list.

In August 1985, the bishop of Galway, Dr Casey sent a letter to all doctors in the Galway area reminding them that sterilisation is 'repugnant to christian teaching'. One month later the sale of another, private, hospital in the area was made subject to the agreement that sterilisations would never be carried out there. The author of that agreement was the same Dr Casey.

A charge often made is that Irish hospitals perform hysterectomies on women for whom female sterilisation would be far more appropriate. Hysterectomy, or the partial/total removal of the womb, involves major surgery and a long stay in hospital. Ethical committees in hospitals can be bypassed by justifying the hysterectomy because of a 'prolapse in (of) the womb'. Irish women are made to endanger their health, undergo major surgery with all its long-term effects because a proper sterilisation service is not available. You can get the service by paying for the right gynaecologist and a private clinic but for most women, the trek to the six counties or Britain is the only option.

Abortion

Abortion is illegal in the twenty-six counties, under the Offences Against the Person Act 1861. A woman who procures an abortion or anyone who helps her to do so can be imprisoned for life. This piece of Victorian legislation was carried unamended into the free state and later into the Republic. Abortion is now unconstitutional. This is the case since the September 1983 anti-abortion referendum, which inserted the 'right to life of the unborn' into the constitution.

It was the alliance of the right which forced through this constitutional amendment, despite the existing severity of legal penalties. They were strongly backed in this campaign by the extreme right in both the medical and the legal professions.

The anti-abortion referendum dominated newspapers, radio and television for a full eighteen months. It proved a shining example of the growing use of moral blackmail in the twenty-six counties. Opponents of the amendment were unambiguously labelled 'murderers', 'whores' and 'sluts'. Only 50% of the population bothered to vote in a campaign backed by the full power of the catholic church unleashed in the pulpits, schools and on the media. The vote was two to one in favour.

Over 10,000 Irish women go to England for abortions every year. These figures cover only those women who give Irish addresses. Going to England for an abortion is an expensive, frightening and lonely experience. In the aftermath of the amendment, the right turned its attention to clinics referring women to England. Open Line Counselling and the Well Woman Centre have been taken to court by the Society for the Protection of the Unborn Child (SPUC). SPUC is attempting to ensure that no Irish woman receives counselling, support or information that might ease her isolation. Right-wing forces have created such a climate of fear and intimidation in this

country that few Irish women have felt able to say they have had an abortion or speak of their experience.

Lesbians and Gay Men

The Offences Against the Persons Act 1861 makes homosexual acts between consenting male adults illegal. Lesbianism is not referred to in this Act. This anomaly is not the result of a more liberal attitude to lesbians but to a denial of women's sexuality. Lesbians and gay men are denied existence by both state and church this country. Media representation is either patronising or more usually sensationalist. Schoolchildren are given almost no information in this area and what there is designed to frighten or repel. Sexual life and sexual love should be both straight and narrow according to the church and the state.

Few lesbians and gay men have been able to

declare their sexuality openly. Sexual repression affects everybody in this society. Towards the gay community it reaches its extreme.

The last ten years have seen the development of gay centres, lesbian groups, emergency telephone lines and gay social events. These are mostly confined to Dublin, Belfast, Derry and Cork. Living in rural areas can mean complete isolation for lesbians and gay men. In the cities, ghettoisation is severe. Breaking through into social and political life is happening, but it is slow and painful. Abuse, harassment and physical violence are common.

Instant dismissal from work is a constant threat for lesbians and gay men. In the recent case in which Eileen Flynn lost her job in a school in Wexford for being pregnant and living with a married man, the precedents cited in the tribunal were cases from England of dismissal over sexual orientation. Sex discrimination legislation does not cover sexual orientation. Attempts to challenge the law in this country have failed at every level. David Norris has now taken the case for homosexual rights to the European Court of Human Rights.

Future Prospects

To assert the right to control your own body or express your own sexual preference means waging a continuous battle against both church and state in Ireland. Concessions have been made, but they are thin on the ground. The church adamantly refuses to provide proper sex education in the many schools it controls. Irish women grow up in guilt and fear of their own sexuality. Sexual relationships between or within the sexes are fraught with distrust and pain. Concealed births, teenage pregnancies, estranged families and damaged personalities are all part of the social fabric of this country. For all the moralising, there is a real lack of human morality and compassion.

The one area where the church will fight to the end to maintain its control is education. Here, the right-wing catholic ideology has its strongest platform. Changes in health services and social practices notwithstanding, the catholic church still has a stranglehold on the lives of children and youth. We all pay the price for their refusal to permit social and sexual choices.

Living on the Edge

Fergus Bourke

More and more people are dependent on the welfare system, north and south of Ireland. Changing economic and social conditions have put increasing pressure on an inadequate system. The most obvious change is the extremely high level of unemployment. The numbers of elderly people have increased as health has improved. There has also been a growth in the number of single-parent families. It's not only welfare claimants who experience hardship. Those on low wages, for example, often live in poverty but do not appear on the statistics. Welfare claimants make up 25% of the adult population in the six counties and about 20% in the twenty-six counties. If you include all their dependants, both adult and children, the proportion shoots up to 35% in the twenty-six counties. In all, 1.22 million people are living on welfare in the twenty-six counties.

The Twenty-Six Counties

There has never been a coherent set of welfare regulations or a single all-embracing piece of legislation in the twenty-six counties. It is a haphazard complex system which has grown up bit by bit over the years. Different regulations cover different claimants, making it highly unwieldy and bureaucratic. This situation has been compounded by the growing numbers dependent on it.

Women and Welfare

Because the welfare system is tied so closely to a rigid model of the traditional family, it is riddled with discrimination. By classifying women as dependants, the welfare system is cheaper to operate: this way fewer women receive direct payments.

Women can be either denied the right to be independent claimants or else refused certain payments. Women with children are virtually excluded from claiming as unemployed unless they have just left the workforce through redundancy or lay-off. The state exploits the fact that, traditionally, married women have taken care of children unpaid in the home. While a father can declare himself unemployed, a mother rarely can. Where the father is not around, women claimants are channelled into insulting categories such as 'deserted wives' and 'unmarried mothers'. Women then find themselves excluded from state employment schemes because they are not registered as unemployed.

While the numbers involved are lower, discrimination against male claimants arises in a different but related manner. The welfare system does not allow for 'unmarried fathers' or 'deserted husbands' only unemployed, sick or elderly men. This assumes the same model of a traditional family with a male head. Fathers looking after and rearing their children have not yet been heard of in the welfare system! Men are channelled into unemployment categories where they may be asked to produce 'evidence' that they are actively seeking employment. Women with children who attempt to claim unemployment assistance are very often asked to produce evidence too, but of a different kind — evidence that childcare arrangements have been made in the event of employment opportunities arising.

	Numbers	% of population
Population of the twenty-six counties	3,443,405	100%
No. of welfare recipients	679,587	20%
No. of welfare dependants	1,223,870	35%

There are over 1.2 million welfare dependants in the twenty-six counties, making up 35% of the population. These figures do not · include those in receipt of children's allowances which can be claimed by all those with children regardless of whether on welfare or not.

The vast majority (81%) of those over sixty-six years of age are on welfare as are the majority (63%) of widows.

The welfare system is divided into **social insurance schemes** and **social assistance schemes.** Social insurance schemes are based on **contributions** paid in, while in the workforce. Eligibility depends on the number and level of contributions and certain additional factors. Social insurance schemes include employment benefit, disability benefit, contributory old age and widows' benefit and maternity benefit. Such schemes are financed from employer and employee contributions and are supplemented by direct government funds.

Social assistance schemes are financed directly by the state and the basis of eligibility for such schemes is a means test. Social assistance schemes include unemployment assistance, unmarried mothers' allowance, deserted wives' allowance and supplementary welfare allowance.

Who Are the Claimants?

The elderly, the unemployed and those claiming family income support make up the vast majority of social welfare claimants. Family income support includes 'unmarried mothers', 'deserted wives', 'prisoners' wives' and others. Unemployed claimants have increased by the greatest numbers. Social welfare expenditure by programme breaks down as follows:

	Expenditure	% of total
Old age pension	**£590,660,000**	28%
Unemployment	**£553,381,000**	27%
Family income support	**£479,174,000**	23%
Illness	**£290,115,000**	14%
Miscellaneous	**£ 79,094,000**	4%
Administration	**£ 83,330,000**	4%
TOTAL	**£2,075,734,000**	

The number of claimants in different areas has grown substantially over the past few years. Between 1975 and 1984, those on unmarried mothers' allowance increased from 2823 to 9238: those on invalidity pensions increased from 10,000 to nearly 22,000: those on unemployment payments increased from 103,316 to 214,162. The following table outlines the number of claimants and their dependants in different categories.

	Elderly	**Widows**	**Deserted wives**	**Unmarried mothers**
Claimants	233,143	90,008	7,790	19,238
Dependants	236,640	113,799	20,744	20,618

	Prisoners' wives	**Disability benefit**	**Invalidity pensions**
Claimants	237	72,120	21,533
Dependants	698	138,975	44,141

	Unemployment benefit	**Unemployment assistance**
Claimants	93,110	103,912
Children	70,113	117,581

The rates of payment for the majority of social welfare allowances and benefits were only marginally increased, by 4%, in the 1986 budget. The government presented this increase as being in line with or just ahead of inflation. But the low rates of payment mean that a 4% increase translates into at most £1–£3 a week.

The rate of unemployment assistance for a single person in long-term unemployment living in an urban area is £36.70 a week from July 1986. A claimant with an adult dependant (usually a man with a wife who is not in paid employment) gets £58.65. A claimant with an adult dependant and three children gets £84.95. This means that **five** people are expected to live on a weekly income of £84.95. Living on welfare in this country means living in poverty, constantly trying to stretch a miserable income to impossible lengths. To make matters worse, those on welfare are constantly subject to a barrage of insults and abuse.

Women on the unmarried mothers' allowance have been singled out for attack recently. Accusations that women deliberately get pregnant just to claim the allowance have been made. In reality, the unmarried mother's allowance for mother **and** child works out at £56.15 per week from July 1986. Hardly a fortune!

One source of hostility is that fact that those in similar circumstances receive different payments. For instance, a claimant on unemployment assistance with **two** children receives £5 less than someone on unmarried mother's allowance with one child. The first child of a woman on deserted wives' allowance gets £11.25 but the first child of someone on unemployment assistance gets £8.15. However crazy this sounds, the welfare system is riddled with such discrepancies. This kind of inequality can turn one group of claimants against others who appear to be getting a 'better deal'. Sorting out this situation and reducing the administrative mess that goes with it could be simply done by equalising rates of those fully dependent on welfare **upwards.** Then, all first children of welfare claimants would be paid at the £11.25 rate. (This does not, of course, resolve the issue that £11.25 is nowhere near enough to feed, clothe and look after a child.)

Another source of conflict for those on welfare is the bitterness felt by many on totally inadequate wages in the economy. It is possible for wages to work out lower than welfare payments.

This is not because welfare payments are high, but because wages are so unacceptably low. It makes little sense to work five days a week for wages that leave you in poverty.

Attacks on welfare claimants often point to the fact that some people on welfare do casual work when they can get it and don't declare it. But, one look at the level of welfare payments is enough to convince anyone that getting work now and again is absolutely essential. Electricity bills have to be paid. Welfare doesn't stretch to the toys at Christmas which are screaming at us from the television, to any bit of a holiday or simply to purchasing the schoolbooks and winter coats for growing children.

JO NESBITT

SOCIAL WELFARE PAYMENTS

Social Assistance Rates

Personal and adult dependant rates	**July '86**
Old age non-contributory pension and blind pension	**Rate** £
— (i) Under 80:	
Personal rate	45.75
Person with adult dependant under 66	68.75
— (ii) 80 or over:	
Personal rate	49.10
Person with adult dependant under 66	72.10
Widows, deserted wives, prisoners' wives:	
Under 66	44.90
66 to 79	45.75
80 or over	49.10
Unmarried mother's allowance (including one child)	56.15
Prescribed relative's allowance	25.60
Unemployment assistance:	
Urban:	
Short duration	
Personal rate	34.05
Person with adult dependant	58.65
Long duration	
Personal rate	36.70
Person with adult dependant	63.15
Rural:	
Short duration	
Personal rate	33.00
Person with adult dependant	56.95
Long duration	
Personal rate	35.50
Person with adult dependant	61.30
Single woman's allowance	39.15
Orphan's non-contributory pension	25.50

Supplementary welfare allowance:	
Personal rate	33.00
Person with adult dependant	56.95
Payment increases for child dependants	
(i) Widows, deserted wives, prisoners' wives:	
Under 66: First child	11.25
Second to fifth child	12.35
Sixth and subsequent children	10.60
Over 66: First child	11.50
Second to fifth child	12.65
Sixth and subsequent children	10.80
(ii) Old age and blind pensioners:	
First child	9.30
Second child	10.50
Third to fifth child	8.15
Sixth and subsequent children	6.50
(iii) Unemployment assistance (short duration) and supplementary welfare allowance recipients:	
First child	8.15
Second child	9.30
Third to fifth child	7.25
Sixth and subsequent children	5.80
(iv) Unemployment assistance (long duration):	
First child	8.70
Second child	9.90
Third to fifth child	7.70
Sixth and subsequent children	6.20

SOCIAL WELFARE PAYMENTS

Social Insurance Rates

Personal and adult dependant rates **July '86**
£

Retirement pension/old age
contributory pension under 80:
—Personal rate 53.45
—Person with adult dependant
under 65 .... 87.55
—Person with adult dependant 66
or over 93.35

Retirement pension/old age
contributory pension 80 or over:
—Personal rate 57.10
—Person with adult dependant
under 66 .... 91.20
—Person with adult dependant 66
or over 97.00

Widow's contributory pension/
deserted wife's benefit:
—Under 66 .... 48.10
—66 to 79 .... 49.10
—80 or over 52.35

Invalidity pension
—Personal rate under 66 .... 47.10
—Personal rate 66 or over 48.05
—Person under 66 with adult
dependant 77.70
—Person over 66 with adult
dependant 79.25

Disability unemployment
benefit: (1)
—Personal rate 41.10
—Person with adult dependant 67.70
Maternity allowance (1) 41.10

Orphan's contributory allowance 30.40

Increases for child dependants
(i)　Widows and deserted wives:
　　Under 66: First child 12.40
　　　Second to fifth child 13.65
　　　Sixth and subsequent
　　　children 11.75
　　Over 66: First child 12.75
　　　Second to fifth child 13.80
　　　Sixth and subsequent
　　　children 12.05
(ii)　Old age and retirement
　　pensioners:
　　　First child 10.60
　　　Second child 11.70
　　　Third to fifth child 9.75
　　　Sixth and subsequent
　　　children 8.00
(iii)　Invalidity pensioners:
　　Under 66: First child 10.45
　　　Second child 11.50
　　　Third to fifth child 9.55
　　　Sixth and subsequent
　　　children 7.75
　　Over 66: First child 10.60
　　　Second child 11.70
　　　Third to fifth child 9.75
　　　Sixth and subsequent
　　　children 8.00
(iv)　Disability and
　　unemployment beneficiaries:
　　　First child 9.40
　　　Second child 10.50
　　　Third to fifth child 8.70
　　　Sixth and subsequent
　　　children 6.95

'Discretion'

One of the key features of the welfare system in the twenty-six counties is the fact that so many of its provisions are administered under the **discretionary** power of social welfare officials. This means that claimants are forced to argue their case, chat-up the face behind the hatch, never get angry and watch their language. There are few occasions where the department puts **on paper** the details of claimant entitlements. The actual ins and outs of the means test which assistance claimants must go through are a mystery even to those who have spent years studying the system.

In effect the welfare system is not based on **rights** but rather on arbitrary decisions by officials to pay out or not. That's not to say that some welfare officials are not sympathetic and actually assist claimants. But too often, hostility from an official can be felt in the air. Discretion should mean that rules are bent to take **need** into account. In this country it usually means that people don't know their entitlements or why they have been granted or denied a particular payment. Sometimes, being assertive works — sometimes you've created an enemy who takes revenge. Fundamentally, the attitude is 'We're doing you a favour and don't have to answer your questions.'

The Appeal System

The social welfare appeals system is a farce. The department gives **no reasons** why claims are rejected. Over 20,000 claims were denied in 1985. No explanations were issued. A claimant shows up for an appeal, without being informed that she or he has a right to be represented and that costs can be covered. It's like going to court without being told the charges, without representation and without receiving a book of evidence from the prosecution. Senator Brendan Ryan is currently sponsoring a private member's bill to establish full rights of appeal and access to information on denied claims. No government has yet seen fit to change the situation.

Finding out your rights is a nightmare in the welfare system. Rather than highlighting the odd case of welfare 'fraud', the whole issue of under-claiming, lack of information, denial of rights under appeal — these are the true scandals of the welfare system.

I WANTED TO GO OUT AND CHANGE THE WORLD BUT I COULDN'T FIND A BABY SITTER !

The Travellers

Few groups in this society have been the object of such inhuman and systematic discrimination as the travellers. Media and particularly newspaper coverage of travellers associates the travelling community with crime and violence — rarely with the poverty, discrimination and prejudice with which travellers are daily confronted. Travellers are regularly refused entry to shops, pubs and every kind of commercial and public place. They are frequently physically ejected from buses, parks, buildings and streets for no apparent reason. This is racism. It occurs despite the fact that this society has consistently refused to provide housing, properly serviced sites, health services and educational facilities to the travelling community.

The numbers of travellers have increased dramatically over recent years according to 'official' statistics. In 1960 there were about 6000 travellers. Now there are over 20,000. The travelling community is no longer one in which everyone is on the road. Some have settled into houses, in estates in Dublin and elsewhere. Others have settled into long-term sites and stopping places. The biggest concentration of travellers is in the Dublin area. Outside Dublin the majority live in the west and south-west in Galway, Cork, Limerick and Kerry and also Wexford in the south-east.

Traditionally, travellers lived on skills like tin-smithing, and could pick up work on a door-to-door basis while travelling in caravans around the country. Seasonal farmwork and fruit picking provided a source of income. As this country became more urbanised, travellers were unable to survive on traditional skills. Some got involved in scrap dealing and selling on roadsides or at markets. Today, most travellers live on the dole or other welfare payments.

Few travellers have had the opportunity to attend school on a regular basis — although this situation has improved over recent years. Demands for sites with proper washing and cleaning facilities have never been responded to by local authorities, who have continuously passed the buck from one to another. Simple requests for hard sites rather than mud-laden

Derek Speirs (Report)

lay-bys have yet to be answered in any but the most piecemeal fashion.

The emergence of the highly organised travellers' movement, Mincéir Misli, has already begun to force concessions from reluctant local authorities.

Mincéir Misli is an organisation of travellers fighting for travellers' rights. It has already broken through the mould of well-meaning but mainly settled community groups speaking for and representing travellers. Travellers have consistently refused to move from sites, like the Tallaght by-pass, until alternative accommodation is provided.

Evictions from so-called unauthorised sites have resulted in travellers losing their possessions. Hostility and prejudice breeds in circumstances where the state has simply refused to provide the accommodation and services which are so desperately needed. Direct battles between travellers and residents of local communities have broken out time and time again, fuelled by the lack of response by housing and other local authorities to the urgent and basic demands of the travelling community.

After years of stalling, Dublin County Council finally agreed to the establishment of thirty sites around County Dublin, holding a maximum of five families each. Some Fianna Fáil councillors opposed the plan, despite the fact that the motion came from their own party. Sites are to be hard-surfaced, with washing and storage facilities, a waste disposal area and landscaping. Eight of the proposed sites are currently in the hands of religious orders. To the justified anger of travellers, sites are to have management committees which include police, clergy, county officials and residents' representatives as well as travellers. Travellers want autonomy for their community and reject these proposed management committees.

Long years of appalling facilities have forced travellers to endure long winters in extremely harsh conditions. Health has been seriously affected as a result. Only 23% of travellers are over thirty years of age and life expectancy is low.

Family size is also way above the average size in the rest of society. Over half of travelling women aged forty-nine or over have had ten or more live births. Infant mortality rates are also way above the national average: the majority of infant deaths are due to respiratory disease. Terrible living conditions are a direct cause of the serious health problems experienced by travellers — conditions for which the state is directly responsible.

Mincéir Misli, the travellers' movement, is not just concerned with sites, education and health. They are demanding recognition for travellers as 'a separate ethnic group, with its own culture, language, values, norms, models, structures'. They completely oppose state policies of integration or absorption of travellers into the settled community. At the very least, they want full rights to organise and manage their own community, backed up by proper sites and full health and educational facilities.

Unemployment

Lack of job opportunities is no new phenomenon in Irish society. Emigration traditionally acted as an outlet for tens of thousands of Irish people who could not get work. Mass emigration from rural Ireland was a feature of the 1950s, as many could no longer look to the land for a livelihood. For a brief period during the 1960s employment grew and emigration was halted. More recently, the international scale of the economic recession meant emigration became less and less of an option. Despite this, emigration has re-emerged over the last few years, especially among young people from Dublin and other areas. It is estimated that around 25,000 people emigrated in 1985 alone.

Unemployment has reached nearly a quarter of a million people in the twenty-six counties alone. The concept of a 'job for life'

are extremely scarce. The other side of this coin is the devastation of the lives of many thousands of young people who have literally never experienced paid employment — and many never will.

In a country where there are only 1.1 million registered employed people, to have nearly a quarter of a million unemployed is frightening and unacceptable. And it is widely recognised that the 'official' figures underestimate the true level of unemployment. Registration and payments are denied to many women with children, to youths aged sixteen to eighteen years and to those over sixty-five. In this society, employment is not only a source of regular income, but also of identity and legitimacy. Such a devastating level of unemployment **marginalises** on a **permanent** basis a growing section of the population, who will never enter or re-enter the mainstream economy.

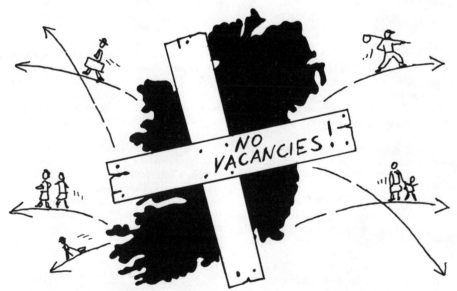

has virtually disappeared and the notion that certain industries provide secure and relatively well-paid work has taken a severe battering.

The Dunlops, Fords, Courtaulds, De Lorean, Rowntrees, Fiat, Sugar Company and other layoffs and closures have seen tens of thousands of skilled workers thrown out of work at an age when new work possibilities

Who Are the Unemployed?

Over half of those who are on the unemployment register are on the **lowest** level of welfare payments, receiving the **minimum** rates of unemployment assistance. Unemployment levels have risen relentlessly since 1979, when it was 85,000, just one-third of its present level of 235,000. Those on the register are on it for longer and longer stretches of time. This means that any insurance coverage they had from periods of employment has run out, forcing them down to minimum payment levels.

Women under twenty-five and men between twenty-five and thirty-five appear most often on the unemployment register. Male unemployment rates are particularly high among those in the building and construction industry. There are 50,000 registered unemployed in this sector alone.

Among women, the crisis in the clothing and footwear industries has meant that higher than average rates are recorded in those sectors.

Youth Unemployment

Nearly one in five of the registered unemployed are under twenty-five years, although payments to young people living with their parents are derisory and often not worth registering for. There are fewer teenagers in the workforce these days, because larger numbers continue within the educational system for longer periods. The unemployment rates among those who are is 32%, about **twice** the national average. The youth unemployment rate jumped dramatically from 15% in 1961 to 32% in 1984. This happened because the teenage population has been growing at a faster rate than the total adult population and there is a dearth of job opportunities in the economy.

Those aged twenty to twenty-four years have also been increasing in numbers at a faster rate than the total adult population. In 1961, 8% of the population was in this age group, now 12% of the population is in this group. Longer time spent in the educational system has had less effect among this age group. 18% of the labour force is aged twenty to twenty-four. Unemployment has escalated rapidly, rising from 6% in 1961 to 18% in 1984, just above the national average.

Groups at Risk

Young people are extremely vulnerable in periods of high unemployment. Employers tend to select those with experience when the job market is so squeezed. Redundancies are generally planned on a 'last in, first out' basis resulting in a high rate of job loss among youth.

Social attitudes favour the 'male bread-winner' and often act against women seeking work. Unskilled workers, among whom women are concentrated, suffer badly because as do older workers whose skills have been displaced by technological changes.

Long-term unemployment has taken hold in this country. Temporary employment schemes break the monotony and provide a marginal improvement in income. But they **are** temporary. They often lack any significant training content and do not resolve the problem of long-term proper paid employment opportunities. The future prospects for employment in this country are bleak.

Those who speak glibly of a 'leisure society' and 'redefining work' fly in the face of social reality. Leisure is only possible where there is work. You can only redefine work when you have work. Setting up your own business, becoming an entrepreneur or defining yourself as self-employed sounds like a good plan. But it is impossible when no capital and little training are available. The long-term unemployed who have been marginalised and demoralised by a society which buries them in figures are the least likely to be in a position to do any of these things. Young people who have never had a day's paid work in their lives are also unlikely candidates. Only through the development of social and political movements can this situation even begin to change. Setting up co-operatives by tapping collective energy usually arises out of political battles fought by organised groups who have resisted factory closures or demanded community facilities.

There is perhaps no indictment of any society so serious as that the creative, productive and imaginative energy of its people is squandered on such a scale.

The six counties

Very high levels of unemployment and widespread poverty mean that increasing numbers of people in the six counties are dependent on an inadequate welfare system.

Just over 25% of the population in the six counties are welfare claimants. This is only one factor in the poverty cycle. Those outside the welfare system are often living in poverty. Wages are particularly low, the majority of women are outside the paid workforce and household size is relatively large. **32% of all households in the six counties live on an income of less than £75 a week.** To make a bad situation worse, the social welfare system in the six counties has been used as a weapon against those who have protested about the political situation.

Payments for Debt Act

The Payments for Debt (Emergency Provisions) Act (Northern Ireland) 1971 is a piece of 'emergency' legislation which applies only to the six counties. It allows direct state interference in people's welfare entitlements. This notorious piece of legislation is still in force in the six counties. It was originally introduced as a piece of 'temporary' emergency legislation by the British state. It's a repressive Act, giving the state the right to **deduct at source** from people's benefits if they are in arrears to public bodies. It was introduced at a time when tens of thousands of people in the six counties were withholding rent and rates as a protest against internment (detention without trial). Not only could money to cover such arrears be compulsorily deducted, but charges could be levied on welfare claimants to cover the cost of collection. Under this same Act, those subject to such deductions could be excluded from 'exceptional needs' payments without any right of appeal.

To use impoverishment as a weapon in such a direct form is an indication of the callous and vindictive nature of British administration in the six counties.

Not only would those who had taken part in the protest be made to pay but their dependants and children would be made to suffer as well. This direct use of the welfare system as part of emergency repressive legislation was a new departure.

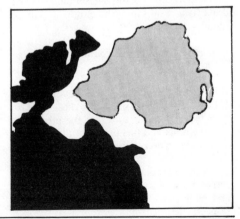

In the late 1970s, while some parts of the operation of the Act were improved, the Act was **retained and extended**. This happened even though both internment and the rents and

Low-paid workers in public employment can have their wages docked at source. Although the maximum deduction is supposed to be £11.45 per week, Eileen

rates strike were over. The extension of the Act meant that deductions could also be made from the wages of public employees in respect of arrears to public bodies. The Act was also extended to encompass fuel debts. The 'high level of debt in northern Ireland' was cited as a 'reason' for extending and retaining the Act. This is untrue: 59% of tenants in the six counties were in arrears in 1982 compared to 68% in Lambeth and 66% in Wandsworth (both London boroughs).

The result of this repressive Act is that the social welfare system in the six counties has effectively become **a mechanism for collecting debts.** This results in pushing more and more families further under the poverty line. In Eileen Evason's study of poverty and unemployment in the six counties **On the Edge** she argues:

> In essence, therefore, the Payments for Debt Act has been used since the latter part of the 1970s to ensure that the province's rising rents and fuel prices result in private hardship rather than public debt.

Eileen Evason points out that deductions can be made at source from all major benefits and allowances, including, in some circumstances, child benefit.

Evason cites a recent case in which £54.81 was deducted from an employee's gross wage of £69.19! It's also evident from cost-of-living data on the six counties that both rent and fuel costs have been rising at a rapid rate. Rents, for example, rose by 26% in 1980, 38% in 1981 and 22% in 1982.

The Belfast Welfare Rights Project documented in its report that just three items — food, fuel and housing — accounted for 75% of the actual income of those living on the poverty line. Fuel costs alone accounted for over 20% of their incomes. Fuel costs in the six counties are particularly high. For instance, gas costs 93.7p per therm in the six counties compared to 40.4p per therm in Britain. The link between the welfare system and debt collection is even more insidious when the high and rising cost of rent and fuel are taken into account.

Supplementary Benefit

The high level of dependence on supplementary benefit in the six counties reinforces the picture of widespread poverty and hardship. Supplementary benefit includes a series of benefits for those in circumstances of **exceptional need.** 22% of the total population of the six counties is dependent on supplementary benefit. A slightly higher percentage

(24%) of the total child population is on supplementary benefit. Nearly half of those claiming supplementary benefit are the unemployed — the other main group of claimants are pensioners. The unemployed can only get the **lower** ordinary rate of benefit. So, in the six counties where dependence on supplementary benefit is heavy, claimants tend to be on the lowest rates. One child in every four is in a claimant family; one child in every six is in a family dependent on the low rate of payment.

Unemployment

The virtual collapse of traditional industries (engineering, ship-building, textiles) as well as extensive closures among newer industries have created an employment wasteland in the six counties. Nearly half of those in work today are in the public sector.

The six counties have consistently recorded the highest rate of unemployment of any area of the EEC. The 'official' rate for 1984 was 21% making more than one in five of the workforce unemployed. The male rate is higher still at 26%. **One in four men in the workforce is unemployed. There are also significant differences in unemployment rates among catholics and protestants in the six counties, reflected in regional variations. The 1971 census showed that two-thirds of the unemployed were catholic, although catholics made up only one-third of the population. The male unemployment rate in August 1985 was 18% in Ballymena (a protestant town) but was 48% in Strabane (a mainly catholic town).**

Unemployment among women has been somewhat lower but it should be remembered that 'official' unemployment registers often exclude women. Many are denied access to the workforce in the first place. Among women in the workforce, many are in the public and private service. This has been a more stable sector than manufacturing.

As in the twenty-six counties, the length of time that people are unemployed is rising all the time. In 1984, over half of those on the register had been there for over a year.

The response by the British state to the political struggle in the six counties has resulted in additional hardship for those living in poverty. Tens of thousands of families have had people imprisoned and interned. Not only does this mean a loss of earnings but also the extra cost of prison visits, parcels and court attendance. Mass raids on communities by the British army leave scores of houses ransacked and torn apart. Repairs to doors, windows, floor boards and furniture are costly and time-consuming. This is to say nothing of the terror and mental stress caused, particularly among younger children.

The Media

The media have become a more and more important part of everyone's lives and young people are growing up in a mass media culture. In the twenty-six counties the media have been a target of direct political interference over the past fifteen years.

We live in an era in which the media have become internationalised. For countries like Ireland, this means domination by British and American culture. Mass-produced western

further undermined over the past few years by a new and powerful development: pirate commercial radio stations. Radio programmes on the state station, Radio Telefis Éireann (RTE), are almost exclusively home-produced but a huge proportion of television programmes is imported.

Some History

News of the easter rising was broadcast inter-

media culture effectively destroys cultural diversity, reducing everything to a coca-cola world where success is measured against Dallas-style soap operas.

Women are portrayed through crass and oppressive media images, both in advertising and television and radio programmes. We are seen as being obsessed with washing, ironing, looking pretty and always coping. Women are always presented as satisfying everyone else's needs — never their own. Men expect pleasure, women supply it. Instructed by male experts, trying to gratify male desires and earn male approval, women are both sex objects and home-makers.

Radio and Television

The state in the twenty-six counties has a monopoly on broadcasting, but in effect this is little more than a **technical** monopoly. The majority of the population has direct access to four British television channels and countless radio stations. The state monopoly has been

nationally by the school of wireless telegraphy from Dublin in 1916. It was ten years later, four years after the establishment of the free state, that Radio Bhaile Átha Cliath (Radio Dublin) was established as a public broadcasting service. Offers from the Marconi company and Lord Beaverbrook (of the **Daily Express**) to do it for us were turned down. In 1932, the radio service went national in time for the eucharistic congress, and by 1938 was broadcasting regularly nationally as Radio Éireann.

Radio Éireann was financed by licence fees and advertising, using a form of sponsored programmes until spot advertising was introduced in 1960. It is estimated that three out of four adults listen to RTE radio every day via its three national channels (Radio 1, Radio 2 and Radio na Gaeltachta) or its local services (Cork local radio and RTE community radio).

Television broadcasting started in 1961 with a single channel, RTE (now RTE 1). It has since expanded with a second channel, RTE 2. RTE is financed through licence and advertising, and it also has commercial interests in the **RTE Guide** (programme guide magazine) and RTE Relays/Dublin Cable Systems, which relays piped (cable) television in the Dublin area. More recently two subsidiaries have been established to produce and market specific programmes such as the film drama 'The Price'. Both these subsidiaries are registered in Britain.

Finance and RTE

RTE spent £74.29 million in 1984. Broadcasting services on radio and television incurred a shortfall of £1.6 million. The **RTE Guide** recorded a surplus of £0.4 million and RTE Relays/Dublin Cable Systems recorded a surplus of £1.1 million. About 38% of total revenue comes from licence fees, which cost £44 per household for black and white and £62 for colour sets.

Advertising revenue amounted to just over £33 million in 1984 (about 44% of total revenue), television advertising showing a growth rate of 16% for that year. Food, household items and drink dominate television advertising. (Tobacco advertising is banned from television.) Programme expenditure (mainly salaries and wages) amounted to £41.6 million of which £31 million went to television, £9.5 million to general radio and less than £1 million to Radio na Gaeltachta.

Imported Programmes on Television

Nearly two-thirds of all RTE television output is made up of imported programmes, mainly (90%) from Britain and America — the other 10% are mostly from Canada and Australia. The same happens in most third world and dependent countries where the industrialised English-speaking west dominates television. By contrast America imports under 2% of its programmes, France 9% and Britain 13%. Broadcasting acts as a powerful means of shaping attitudes and behaviour and imposing culture and lifestyles. Anglo-American programmes dominate children's viewing in particular, where 78% of programmes are imported.

90% of the RTE budget goes on wages and fixed costs. This leaves only a tiny amount for home-produced programmes. Most of these are current affairs, children's programmes and light entertainment.

There are hardly any regional programmes on television. The percentage of time allotted to programmes in Irish is less than 3% — a tiny proportion and a source of justified anger. Conradh na Gaeilge, who monitor the falling percentages of programmes in Irish, highlight a drop from over 6% in 1970 to only 5% today. This amounts to about four and a half hours of Irish language programmes over one week on RTE 1 and 2. The census of population results show that about 30% of the population speaks Irish. RTE's own research shows that the viewing population for programmes in Irish is between 600,000 and 700,000. Research by the Irish Language Institute showed that over two-thirds of the adult population **favour** Irish language programmes. At present such programmes are mainly news, current affairs, and talk shows, restricting viewers to a very narrow interest range.

A major political battle in Wales succeeded in securing a specific Welsh channel for a viewing population estimated at around 125,000 people.

The cash budget for RTE drama is just £300,000 or **less than 1% of its total expenditure.** This amount of finance could cover two

low-budget television films or six months of the popular drama series 'Glenroe'. Proper funding would not only act as a source of employment for Irish actors, technicians and directors but would also provide for the cultural expression of issues and themes relevant to Irish people. For a culture to survive, it needs a link with its past, and the means to develop and explore new themes and changing realities. RTE is not providing this kind of opportunity.

Over the last couple of years, co-productions, in association with Channel 4, the BBC, a French broadcasting company and London Weekend television have provided a means to put out 'The Year of the French', a number of televised dramas and series such as 'The Price'. Co-productions effectively stretched the available budget last year to around £12 million. However, co-productions are limited to films, dramas and series of a kind that is of interest to the **co-producer.** Effectively, co-production means that whether a programme will **sell abroad** is the critical question. There have been many voices raised over the way in which Ireland and the Irish were portrayed in 'The Price', highlighting the potential problems associated with co-production. **Co-production clearly is not a SUBSTITUTE for a strong budget allotted to fully home-produced drama,** though **alongside** such a budget, it could make sense.

Cheaper but not Better

The cost of home-produced programmes varies considerably according to the type of programme, but all are more expensive than buying in imported programmes. A half-hour of 'Today Tonight' costs about £2200, the Late Late Show costs about £3000 an hour, while a major drama costs up to £40,000 an hour. By contrast, imported programmes cost on average between £900 and £1200 an hour.

Foreign news is bought into RTE through the European News Exchange, a service provided by the Eurovision Broadcasting Union. Outside broadcasting is particularly costly — an outside broadcast unit to cover a football match in Croke Park costs £1 million to purchase.

Every performer is paid a fee, but artists' fees account for only 8% of expenditure. Copyright fees to authors, poets and writers for the use of material accounts for a further 10% of expenditure, and travel accounts for about another 5% of the budget.

Sex Segregation

RTE employs about 2000 people with a range of skills. About 30% of RTE employees are women. The report of the joint committee on women's rights produced a report in 1985 on the portrayal and position of women in the media.

82% of workers in RTE in clerical, secretarial or administrative jobs are women. These are the low-paid, low-status jobs with little or no impact on media production. Over half of all women in RTE are stuck in these work areas. In 1984, **twice as many** male as female applicants to the station got jobs, though the same number of men and women applied.

RTE, as a state owned broadcasting organisation, reflects the blatant sexism that prevails throughout the social and political strands of Irish society.

To quote Emily O'Reilly, **Sunday Tribune** 20 April 1986:

> **RTE's agricultural correspondent is a man. The financial correspondent is a man. The economics correspondent is a man. The industrial correspondent is a man. The**

political correspondent is a man. The foreign editor is a man. The European correspondent is a man. The religious affairs correspondent is a man. The Northern editor is a man. All the regional correspondents are men. The head of news is a man. The deputy head of news is a man. The chief subs are men. The deputy editor is a man. The head of Radio na Gaeltachta is a man. The head of news features is a man. The deputy head of news features is a man. The two assistant editors of news features are men. The head of Radio 2 news is a man. The head of current affairs is a man.

All the controllers of programmes and deputy controllers of programmes are men. RTE is an equal opportunities employer.'

—SORRY, BUT WE ALREADY HAVE ONE LADY REPORTER

Pirate Radio

There are about seventy pirate or illegal radio stations across the country — about thirteen in the Dublin area alone. The majority are commercial stations playing pop music all day. News items are usually picked up from newspapers or RTE. One of the biggest, Radio Nova, went out of business in March 1986, but some of its equipment was bought by a new station, Zoom 103.

Sunshine Radio and Radio Q102 are the biggest in Dublin at present — Sunshine says that 25% of those in the fifteen-to-thirty-four group in the Dublin area listen to them every day. Q102 say they get 28% of young Dublin listeners, and Nova used to record a 30% listening figure. Such listening rates compare with a 13% youth listening rate for RTE Radio

2 and an average of 15% for the rest of the pirates in the Dublin areas.

Few moves have been made to close down these stations other than occasional seizures of equipment. The government is planning its own local radio bill based on a two-tier system of commercial and community-based independent local radio stations. The battle over the airwaves is intense. Religious groups, RTE and existing pirates are vying for control. Licensing is likely to be marked by the patronage system, which is such a familiar feature of the Irish political scene. Very few of the pirates are unionised at present and the majority of music played is either British or American. Advertising is extensive. Community-based local radio is liable to suffer from a lack of resources and facilities as advertising revenue gets channelled into commercial ventures.

Advertising

By law, only 10% of air time can be allocated to advertising — about seven and a half minutes an hour on television. There are fifty-eight minutes of advertising time on television every day which is high compared to France with fifteen minutes a day, the Netherlands with twenty-one minutes and Germany, Austria and Switzerland with twenty minutes. Advertisers in Ireland spend a higher percentage of their budget on television advertising (42%) compared to 31% in America or 29% in Britain. The report on women in the media showed that 54% of ads surveyed portrayed women as 'decorative females', 24% as home-makers and just 4% as working in the economy.

Censorship — Section 31

Section 31 of the Broadcasting Authority Act (1960) gives the government, via the minister for communications, the right to prevent

particular items being broadcast. Using section 31 the entire RTE authority was sacked in 1972 following a broadcast of a report of an interview with Seán Mac Stíofáin, a republican militant and leader. The journalist who carried out the interview spent a week in jail after a three month order by the special criminal court for contempt of court. He refused to reveal his sources.

In 1976, an amendment to the Act was brought in which gave the minister the right to ban anything which 'tends to undermine the authority of the state'. In addition, a statutory order was brought in under section 31 in 1977, prohibiting members of republican organisations from appearing on the airwaves. Interviews with members of the **legal** organisation Sinn Féin **even where they are elected representatives** were also prohibited. So, while Sinn Féin and IRA spokespersons are heard on British radio and television and broadcast across the country, RTE is forbidden to carry such interviews.

The breadth of section 31 allows it to be used against any individual or organisation considered a 'threat' to state authority. New orders under section 31 can be introduced at any time. Journalists, following the events of 1972, operate in a climate of fear and are often forced into self-censorship. Trade unions and other organisations have been denied broadcasting access for their spokespersons because they also happen to be members of Sinn Féin. This occurs even when the issue under discussion is simply wages or prices. More recently, a representative of NORAID (an American based organisation which raises funds for the Republican Movement) was stopped from appearing on a current affairs programme by the director general of RTE.

It is not just particular people who are prohibited from going on air, but specific remarks or film may be cut. Interviews with anyone who **supports** 'armed struggle' against the British in the six counties are not used.

An RTE crew was ordered to use silent film in 1977 while covering a confrontation between police and protestors outside Portlaoise prison where a hunger strike was taking place. The resulting film was unusable and BBC and ITN film had to be used. A remark referring to Zimbabwe saying 'guerilla movements always win in the end' was cut out of an interview in 1976.

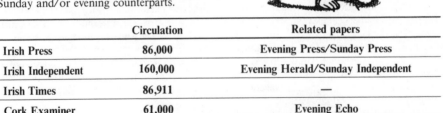

Newspapers

There are four national daily newspapers in the twenty-six counties, three of which publish Sunday and/or evening counterparts.

	Circulation	Related papers
Irish Press	86,000	Evening Press/Sunday Press
Irish Independent	160,000	Evening Herald/Sunday Independent
Irish Times	86,911	—
Cork Examiner	61,000	Evening Echo

In addition there are the **Sunday Tribune,** the **Sunday World** and **Anois** (Irish language Sunday paper). Traditionally, the **Irish Press** has been linked to the Fianna Fáil party and the **Irish Independent** to Fine Gael. **The Irish Times** has been associated with a liberal tradition in the twenty-six counties. The **Independent** newspapers are the most powerful newspaper group, controlling as they do a number of provincial papers in addition to the national ones.

Cartoon/Tom Mathews

Ireland has a very high rate of newspaper readership and a strong tradition of provincial papers, most of which cover local political, sporting and cultural events on a weekly basis. There are over forty provincial newspapers in the twenty-six counties.

A dramatic change has taken place in newspaper readership over the past decade. British tabloid dailies have established a strong foothold, particularly in urban areas. Together, the **Daily Mirror,** the **Star,** and the **Sun** are estimated to sell around 130,000 papers daily in the twenty-six counties. This accounts for about 30% of newspapers consumed every day. The **Mirror** is estimated to sell about 60,000 while the **Sun,** which has recently re-entered the Irish market, claims to sell about 30,000. The recent launching of a new tabloid, *Today,* in Britain has intensified competition in the industry, particularly where new and expanding markets like Ireland are concerned.

There are forty-one provincial newspapers in the twenty-six counties, about half of which were established in the second half of this century. The average circulation of a provin-

cial newspaper has risen from nearly 11,000 in 1974 to over 13,500 today. Research carried out by C. O'Neill at the NIHE Dublin shows that most provincial papers are owned by private limited companies or family firms. It is not unusual for the editor to be a company director also. Between two and sixteen journalists are employed on any one provincial paper. Some of the companies which own provincial papers own more than one.

Competition for advertising from pirate radio stations has put pressure on provincial newspapers. Many are seriously considering taking a stake in or getting involved in local or commercial radio in addition to their newspapers.

There are only **two** publicly owned companies involved in newspapers, the Connaught Tribune Ltd., and Independent

119

Newspapers Ltd. Independent Newspapers Ltd. is the most powerful company involved with the press in the twenty-six counties. It controls about 40% of national daily newspaper circulation and about 57% of Sunday newspaper circulation. In addition, **eight** provincial papers are owned by Independent Newspapers Ltd., accounting for over 13% of the total circulation of the provincial press. Of the other forty firms involved in the provincial press, none controls more than 2% of total circulation.

Independent Newspapers is the **twelfth** biggest company in the twenty-six counties and controls a critical area of the media. Tony O'Reilly is the main figurehead in Independent Newspapers Ltd. He is a director of the newspaper group as well as of Fitzwilton Ltd., which owns nearly 23% of the newspaper company shares. Four of the directors of Independent Newspapers Ltd. are also directors of Fitzwilton Ltd., controlling 31.68% of the company shares. Combined with the Fitzwilton Ltd. shares this amounts to 54.38% of all shares, a full controlling interest in Independent Newspapers Ltd. This is the most powerful private capital interest in the Irish media.

Newspapers are suffering from a declining level of advertising revenue as a result of competition from other areas of the media. In 1979, over 52% of advertising budgets went to newspapers — now less than 30% of advertising comes their way.

New Media

New companies have sprung up in the area of video production and distribution over the last few years. For a country renowned for tight censorship of books and film, video distribution has a free rein. Attempts to control the circulation of 'video nasties' have not yet turned into legislation. Funding for video production suffers from the lack of support which dogs all home-produced media and arts.

The Arts

The twenty-six counties have one of the lowest fundings for the arts of any European country. One of the consequences of this is that many Irish artists get 'adopted' and integrated by the arts in other countries, particularly England. Irish writers like Elizabeth Bowen and Kate O'Brien are considered by most English people to be English. Pat Murphy's film, **Anne Devlin** was listed as British at a recent international conference. Irish poets get included in anthologies of British poetry. Even Bob Geldof has been claimed as a 'true Brit' by Maggie Thatcher herself. Emigration among artists of all kinds has always been high, **both** to avoid censorship and to get support for their work.

The last few years have seen a mini-explosion in all kinds of community-based arts. Funding from temporary employment schemes has breathed life into this area at least in the short term, but many exciting projects are threatened with closure as funding dries up. A recent example of this is the Raised Eyebrow Theatre Group, whose special emphasis is on promoting women's work, women's issues and women's lives and whose existence is now threatened because of lack of funding. Another new development has been a breakthrough of women writers into publishing, having been denied such outlets for decades. There is huge interest in the arts but little support or finance to speak of.

Arts Funding

The major agency involved in funding the arts in the twenty-six counties is the Arts Council. The council gets a grant of just over £5 million from central government funds. In addition, government departments are sometimes involved in arts funding. The Department of Labour funds employment and training schemes in the arts. Private sponsorship of specific events is also a critical source of arts funds.

It is estimated that at least 600 people are employed in the arts. Organisations supported by the Arts Council raised £7 million in revenue from other sources, in addition to their allocations from the council itself in

1984. This means that for every £1 allocated by the council, sponsored organisations raised on average, an additional £1.28. This does not include fund-raising activities by organisations which are not sponsored by the Arts Council.

In February 1986, the Arts Council announced that **no** grants would be paid this year to touring theatre and annual festivals. This was announced after a budget allocation to the Arts Council of £5.7 million rather than the £13 million which they had looked for. This move meant that funding for whole areas of community or national performances has been cut. Major annual events such as the Dublin Theatre Festival, the Wexford opera Festival and the Cork International Choral and Folk Dance Festival were thrown into crisis, forced to seek scarce private sponsorship. The Dublin and Wexford festivals eventually got a once-off grant from the Ireland Fund. The National Theatre Touring Agency announced that it was 'finished', following the loss of funding to professional touring theatre. Total cuts are estimated at around £380,000. Some areas did manage to get increased funds. The budget allocation to film was increased by 20% covering individual project awards as well as film societies.

The general breakdown of Arts Council funding is as follows:

Literature	5%
Visual arts	9%
Film	2%
Drama	46%
Dance	7%
Traditional arts	2%
Music	5%
Opera	4%
Arts centres & festivals	5%
Regions	3%
Community arts	1%
Arts in education	1%
Capital	1%
Administration	9%
	100%

The Abbey Monopoly

The above breakdown shows a clear emphasis on drama — nearly half of the total budget of the Arts Council, about £2.5 million, goes to drama. The lion's share of this, nearly £1.5 million goes to the Abbey Theatre, so about one-quarter of the Arts Council budget goes to the Abbey Theatre. The Druid Theatre company got £105,000 in 1984 and the Centre for the Performing Arts in Dublin got £180 (yes £180). This is a clear example of the monopolisation of funds within the arts by particular organisations.

During 1984 Arts Council grants amounted to £4 million. Grant-aided arts organisations raised additional funds as follows:

Arts Council grants	£4 million
Earnings	£5.2 million
Sponsorship	£0.7 million
Other state funding	£0.7 million
Local authorities	£0.2 million
Other	£0.3 million
TOTAL	£11.1 million

Arts Council grants represented 39% of the income of grant-aided organisations.

A Temporary Boost

A new development in arts funding has gained rapidly in importance in the last year or so. The Department of Labour, through its funding of youth and temporary employment schemes, funded nearly £2 million worth of cultural activities in 1985. This represents almost one-third of the total budget of the Arts Council. However, a cut in the Teamwork budget from £8 million to £5 million is already seriously affecting this area of funding. The Teamwork scheme funded about £700,000 worth of arts employment in 1985. Many theatre companies, community arts programmes and arts centres will be unable to continue to employ people as a result of this cut.

The abysmally low level of Arts Council funding has forced many organisations to rely on temporary and youth employment schemes, despite the low-paid and short-term nature of such employment and funding.

As well as the £700,000 under the Teamwork scheme, over £1 million came through the Social Employment Scheme in 1985. Dependence on such schemes creates serious problems for long-term projects.

The City Workshop Theatre, for example, reached a peak in success and popularity only to face a cut-off in its grant. These schemes limit an individual's employment to one year. City Workshop had to disband at a critical point in its development. Many groups have faced or do face similar problems, as few are in a position to secure long-term funding when the schemes close. Arts centres, which have used such schemes to employ people, also face a crisis over the next two years.

Community arts have been particularly vulnerable to the problems of piecemeal and short-term funding. Clearly, Department of Labour temporary employment schemes are no substitute for adequate arts funding. The crisis for touring theatre, community arts, arts centres and festivals is mounting steadily. The level of funding to the Arts Council is

Derek Speirs (Report)

laughable. Increased funding must be accompanied by a spread of funding across the arts, including regional and community projects and organisations. Many of those involved in the arts have argued that the Arts Council should have resigned after the 1986 budget rather than play around with an outrageously low budget, consequently axing festivals and touring theatres. Such a move, many feel, would have proved more productive in the long run.

Some artists have attacked the elitist and self-perpetuating nature of established arts organisations. Margaretta D'Arcy has singled out AOSDÁNA for attack, decrying its undemocratic and self-satisfied nature. AOSDÁNA is a state-sponsored professional organisation of artists — those elected to its council receive an annual grant of £5000. Many of those in receipt of such grants are also employed in newspapers, RTE and other organisations.

Those in real need find it extremely difficult to break into this closed and undemocratic organisation, says Margaretta.

Film

Irish cinema dates from the early years of this century. The first cinema, **The Volta,** opened in Mary St., Dublin, in 1909, with James Joyce as manager. One year later the first fiction film to be shot in Ireland, **The Lad from old Kerry,** was made by an American production company, Kalem. By 1916, there were about 150 cinemas and halls showing films, including thirty-three in Belfast and twenty-seven in Dublin. Around the same time the Film Company of Ireland was formed and began making Irish films, using mainly Abbey actors. In 1917, Irish Events began to produce regular newsreels on political developments, one of which was made into a feature length

Man of Aran

film on Sinn Féin. It was eventually seized by British troops from a Drogheda cinema.

After the establishment of the free state in 1922, the Censorship of Film Act was one of the first pieces of legislation introduced — it was passed in 1923. It provided for the appointment of a film censor, who could refuse a certificate for a film where it was deemed to be 'indecent, obscene or blasphemous' or 'would be subversive to public morality'. This Act was later extended to cover displays outside cinemas. Hundreds of films were banned or cut in the first year after this Act came into force.

The introduction of sound films in the 1930's boosted cinema attendance and by 1933 700,000 weekly cinema admissions, worth £1.5 million were recorded. **Man of Aran** made by Robert Flaherty in 1932 is one of the most famous early Irish films. It was one of the first sound films made here. By 1935, there were over 180 cinemas operating in Ireland. About 75% of all films shown were from America, with the remaining 25% from Britain. Discontent with the lack of a national film industry gathered momentum, partly expressed through catholic church representatives who feared the influence of 'alien' ideology.

During World War II, 'emergency powers' restricted films which could give offence to a 'friendly' foreign power. 358 films were banned and a further 1139 were cut under these powers. In 1943 a National Film Institute was set up with the assistance of the Department of Industry and Commerce, and with the backing of the catholic church, but without funding. Cinema admissions continued to rise reaching over 50 million by 1955.

In 1958, Ardmore Studios was established with a grant of £45,000 and a £217,000 loan. Their early productions were based on Abbey plays and Abbey actors. During the 1960s film attendances began to drop — Telefis Éireann was broadcasting from 1961. Ardmore went bankrupt in 1964, and was eventually bought by a British company. However, in 1974 RTE bought back Ardmore at a time when film makers in Ireland were doing advertisements to survive. In 1975, the National Film Studios

was set up and the Arts Council began funding film-making on a limited scale.

Film Distribution

Film distribution in the twenty-six counties is under the virtual monopoly of the Ward-Anderson group. They operate through the simultaneous showing of films, of which they have several copies, across the country, saving on both advertising and promotion. The Ward-Anderson group controls about sixty cinemas in all; the Savoy, the Ambassador, the Regent, the Odeon, the Screen, the Green and the Plaza in Dublin and almost all provincial outlets. The Carlton and the Adelphi are controlled by Thorn/EMI. The Association of Independent Cinema Owners includes the Curzon, the Cameo, the Classic and the Bray Twins. They have major problems in getting access to money-making films and have been in severe crisis over the past few years.

A public inquiry concerning monopoly arrangements between the Green Group (Ward/Anderson) who then controlled forty cinemas and foreign distribution companies was held in 1977. Allegations of monopoly practices were denied, and eventually the inquiry accepted this denial. The independent cinema owners, however, have repeatedly stated that they are denied distribution of films which would ensure their financial survival.

This near monopoly situation over film distribution and the traditionally rigid and repressive attitude of the film censor was the background for a new development in the 1970s. Between 1924 and 1980, the film censor banned 3000 films and 8000 others were cut. Film societies, which avoided the censor through a private membership system, sprang up around the country. Societies often showed foreign films and others which would normally never reach the commercial cinema screens. By 1979, the Federation of Irish Film Societies had thirty-six member societies with 7000 members. The Irish Film Theatre had a further 7000 members. In recent years, membership of film societies has fallen off as the censor has been less restrictive. Multi-channel television has also given direct access to many films which would formerly have only been available through the societies. The majority of societies and members today are outside the Dublin area.

Distribution of Irish films suffers in a number of ways. Very few copies are available, so simultaneous distribution cannot happen. Only two copies of the film **Anne Devlin** were available, so distribution was a long-drawn-out and staggered process. Also, many Irish films are 16mm because this is a cheaper type of film, but it tends to be less popular with distributors.

As a result, the 'Irish' film industry most of the time means the shooting of American and English films in Ireland, using the landscape and technicians as it suits them. Irish film-makers have got little state support and have to rely on piecemeal and inadequate finance.

Despite this, many films have been produced about Ireland and in some cases made in Ireland. **Anne Devlin** is the first fully-owned, financed and produced Irish film. It was made by Pat Murphy, a woman who has managed to break the near total male monopoly on film in this country. Up until the 1960s most Irish film-making consisted of documentaries. Yet many Hollywood films have dealt with Irish themes. Irish people attended the cinema in huge numbers in the 1930s, 1940s and 1950s in the face of both catholic church hostility and strict censorship.

The Future

The explosion in all kinds of arts activities from writing to theatre to dance can be seen as an exciting and powerful desire for creativity and expression in a time of economic and political depression. The increasing involvement of women and young people is a demonstration of how those who get excluded from the mainstream arts can and will break through those barriers. There is an enormous fringe full of life developing across the twenty-six counties. But the monopoly over shrinking funds is causing terrible problems. How long can energy and enthusiasm be sustained without support? How many valuable projects will go to the wall while governments pour money into short-term and rigid areas of job creation? Immediate action is needed to support a much wider area of arts activity in this society, if this crucial outlet for creativity is not to be stifled.

The Environment — Natural and Social

Ireland is sold in the tourist brochures for its physical beauty and unspoiled coastline. These days, concern over the environment is mounting. The brochures need rewriting.

Pollution in the Dublin area has reached an extremely serious level. Rivers and lakes have been heavily contaminated by the dumping of industrial and agricultural toxic wastes. The pumping of radioactive waste into the Irish Sea from the British nuclear reprocessing plant at Windscale/Sellafield has turned it into the most radioactive sea in the world.

But the physical or natural environment is not the only cause for concern. The state of the roads, the dereliction of inner city areas, the destruction of historical buildings, and the construction of satellite housing estates all affect our quality of life. This social environment is critical to our physical and emotional well being. Those living in the declining inner city areas or the wastelands of some newer housing estates are most often those at the lower income levels of society. Access to a decent environment is directly tied to your class position. Segregation of social classes into different areas became a feature of this society, as more and more people moved to urban areas.

Physical and Natural Environment

The Dublin area has become increasingly hazardous to live in. Dublin children have significantly more lead in their bodies than children in rural areas. The worst affected areas are Rathmines and Ballyfermot. Most of the lead comes from petrol — about 60%. High levels of lead in the body affect the nervous system and are considered to contribute directly to a deterioration in the mental ability of children. Government regulations have reduced lead levels, but do not yet ensure that cars use lead-free petrol. This would involve modification of cars being sold in this country as such regulations have been introduced in most European countries.

Another major factor contributing to the pollution in the Dublin area is the burning of coal in open fires. Between 1984 and 1985, there was a 50% increase in the smog level in Dublin. The majority of houses built by Dublin corporation use open fires for heating. Monitoring of smog levels was carried out in Trinity College Dublin during the period 11 November to 11 December 1985. On eight of the thirty-one days, smoke levels rose **above** the EEC guideline of 150 micrograms per cubic metres. **The EEC LIMIT of 250 micrograms per cubic metre was exceeded on five out of thirty-one days.** According to the World Health Organisation, levels over 500 micrograms per cubic metre can cause **serious health problems.** Smog levels crossed this limit on **two days,** 4 and 27 November 1985.

The coal industry is an extremely powerful lobby. To reduce households' dependence on coal alone and encourage the use of combined heating systems, the government would have to fund conversion programmes. The smoke which causes smog is produced by the incomplete burning of certain elements in ordinary coal. This happens when coal is burnt in an open fire. Only one-quarter of its useful energy is turned into heat while the rest literally goes up the chimney as smoke. A back-boiler can increase efficiency substantially. The coal industry has a vested interest in blocking any moves towards the use of **less profitable** (though more expensive) smokeless fuel like anthracite. The government does little to improve the situation.

It is not just those in central areas who suffer. Dublin Corporation monitoring showed that the EEC daily limit was breached during 1984/85 no fewer than 124 times in different parts of the city. The highest smoke concentration was recorded in Ballyfermot at 884 micrograms per cubic metre.

This level is way above the world health organisation 500 micrograms ceiling for

serious health problems.

In many ways, the pollution question boils down or burns down to economics. Conversions and combined heating systems are not feasible for most people without government grants. A new product on the British market, 'coalite', a 'smokeless coal' is being sold at 35% dearer than ordinary coal. How can low-income or unemployed people and welfare dependants, the ones who need to use it the most, afford to buy clean fuel?

Acid Rain

The build-up of pollution in the Dublin area has created an 'acid rain' problem. The stone of many of the oldest Dublin buildings is deteriorating rapidly — just look at the blackened stone of Trinity College. The main source of this kind of air pollution damage is the emission of sulphur dioxide (SO_2) into the atmosphere. This is done mainly by power stations and industries. It becomes particularly damaging when it combines with the water in rainfall forming sulphuric acid or 'acid rain'. But it is not all home-produced: we also get the blow-back from Britain.

The take-up of natural gas by Guinness, bakeries, office blocks and hospitals recently has contributed to a reduction in locally produced SO_2 levels. However, the new Moneypoint plant in Co. Clare will be pumping SO_2 into the air, affecting Dublin and the country as a whole. This plant could have had a system of cleaning up its emissions built in during construction. Shortsighted ESB policy has left it without safeguards. Prevailing westerly winds and the wet Irish climate have led many to predict that Moneypoint emissions will produce more 'acid rain' for Dublin.

The Irish Sea

Radioactive waste is regularly discharged into the Irish Sea from Sellafield (formerly Windscale) in Cumbria in Wales. In addition, there are eighteen nuclear reactors along the west coast of Britain. Any accident, such as the recent Chernobyl disaster, would be potentially devastating — the effect incal-

culable. The Sellafield (Windscale) plant is the largest recorded source of radioactive discharge in the world. And it goes straight into the Irish sea. Radioactive traces from Sellafield have been identified in fish as far away as Sweden.

Monitoring of radioactive discharges has been completely underfunded in this country. The budget of the Nuclear Energy Board (NEB) which is responsible for monitoring radioactivity, is £300,000. Twenty-two people are employed; about 12 are technical/ scientific workers. Rainwater and seaweed on the east coast are checked. There is no systematic monitoring of milk, air or marine life, obvious in the aftermath of Chernobyl. The NEB was set up to **promote** nuclear energy, not to protect people's health.

There is a strong feeling that the NEB simply accepts everything the British nuclear industry says. Studies have associated Sellafield discharges (particularly a fire in the 1950s) with a higher than average rate of Downs syndrome births in the Dundalk area. But monitoring is only one part of the problem. Sellafield is unsafe and has a dreadful record of accidents. Dr Robert Blackith, associate professor of zoology at Trinity College Dublin, describes Sellafield as 'inherently unsafe' and its management as 'incompetent'. His view is that 'nothing can be done to make Sellafield safe except to close it down.'

Rural Pollution

Pollution is by no means confined to the Dublin area. Lough Sheelin in Cavan was destroyed for years by agricultural waste (pig slurry). Rivers, particularly in Cork, have regularly had fish killed as a result of the

dumping of toxic wastes.

In Tipperary, a local farmer took the Merck Sharpe & Dohme chemical plant to court looking for compensation for the many unexplained deaths and deformed births among his cattle. He lost his case and is currently appealing that verdict. Environmental damage is notoriously hard to prove. The Avoca valley in Wicklow has been described by Trinity College scientists as 'one of the most lifeless rivers in Europe'. Avoca was destroyed by mining deposits and the pollution from the NET fertiliser plant in Arklow.

Over 30,000 tons of toxic waste are produced in this country every year. There is no record of where the majority of such wastes go. It used to be exported to Britain, but there, public opposition to toxic dumps has curtailed toxic waste importation. The government operates no control over the growing volume of toxic wastes. The scale of the problem has escalated because of growing chemical industries, mainly owned by international companies. The widespread use of chemicals in agriculture and industry is also a factor. There is no doubt that at least some of these wastes are simply being **dumped** into rivers and lakes in the middle of the night. They certainly are not all being stored or exported for treatment. The government can provide no records of the destination of the 30,000 tons which they admit is annually produced. There has been some speculation that the lack of regulation acts as an added attraction to multi-national chemical plants moving into Ireland.

The Social Environment

The social environment, particularly in urban areas, reflects class divisions and inequalities. Segregation of different groups of people into physically distinct areas amounts to a form of **social apartheid,** particularly evident in the Dublin area. The unemployed, welfare dependants and those on low wages are separated into Corporation flats and housing estates across Dublin, many of which have gone into severe decline over the past two decades. On the outskirts of the city, Dublin Corporation has rehoused inner city dwellers along with new households in sprawling housing estates without facilities.

Traditionally, class divisions in Dublin were reflected in the split of working class housing to the north of the Liffey. The middle classes were carefully cosseted on the southside. The growth of Dublin has altered this pattern, although not completely. An enormous sprawl of housing stretches from north Dublin right across the west and south-west of the city. For the most part, these areas are made up of rows and rows of identical houses, with no commercial centres, few community facilities and no planned green areas. They are teeming with young children and teenagers. Public transport to these satellite housing estates is extremely bad. Hundreds of thousands depend on a tiny number of buses on very few routes.

The development of Dublin shows the drive of the profit motive. Corporation housing policy reflects a concern with settling the greatest possible numbers at the cheapest cost with little attention to living conditions. The houses went up, the people moved in, but the promised facilities never materialised. In Tallaght, the original plans included shopping centres, swimming pools, cinemas, parks, community centres, and a rapid rail system. Few of these have been built and those that have came after a long struggle by the local community.

Unemployment and overcrowding are concentrated in some areas: the inner city and local authority estates on the fringe. This over-concentration of young married couples into certain areas denies some communities the vibrancy of contact with people of different ages and social situations.

Ballymun, for instance, now houses mainly single-parent families. Middle-class suburbs are often exclusively professional, business and public sector workers. And never the twain do meet. Mixed areas are largely unknown in Dublin.

The poorest sections of society are literally hidden from view. The middle and upper classes can commute to their southside offices and back out again **without any contact** with the hundreds of thousands living in hardship in the city and county areas.

Contrasting Mount Merrion and Ballymun gives the following results:

	Occupation	%
Mount Merrion	Professional	50%
	Managerial & administration	33%
	Blue collar	10%
	Unemployed	5%
Ballymun	Blue collar	50%
	Lower white collar	18%
	Unemployed	25%

The physical division of Dublin mirrors a social division which means that the most privileged perpetuate their privilege. Neither division looks like a passing phenomenon. (**The Irish Times** 22 October 1985.)

The social environment of Dublin is planned not only to segregate social classes and act as a means of social control, but also to service primarily the private car. The whole organisation of Dublin city gives the car centre stage. Bus and bike lanes are a recent and scarce phenomenon. For those who are outside the car society, the city is virtually an alien environment. There are **two** pedestrianised streets in Dublin city centre, and even there you must watch for trucks and lorries.

For women this is devastating. Dragging children and parcels through car-congested streets is a daily nightmare. Shopping centres have neither changing areas nor play areas. Getting prams and go-carts on and off buses is a physical trial. The elderly desperately cling to the scarce supports in buses that hurtle through traffic. Surely they were designed for some other species!

If ever a city developed without thought for those who live in it, then Dublin must fit the bill. Public transport stops at 11.30 p.m., yet the city centre is where most people have to go for entertainment. After midnight, except at weekends, the city is dead. Everyone has been dispersed to the outskirts. The living communities of Dublin's inner city have been decimated while its residents have been rehoused on the outer fringes of the sprawling city.

Brian Fitzgerald

Opposition to this kind of inhuman development has had some results. Some new inner city housing has been built in the Liberties and City Quay areas. New grants for redevelopment along the quays and around the Custom House area have been announced, but many people feel that it is too little and too late. Unsightly office blocks have already been erected on the remains of Viking Dublin. Georgian squares have been deliberately allowed to fall into disrepair and decay by speculators who have no interest in conservation. There are derelict sites all over the city centre. Acres of car parks have replaced living communities. Reversing the trend involves large-scale investment and redevelopment.

Housing Policy

Government housing policy is oriented towards home ownership in the twenty-six counties. Three-quarters of the population lives in private housing. Few have been able to buy their houses outright. The majority spend decades on the mortgage system. Repaying a house loan is a lifetime's work. At least the tax system subsidies those on mortgages, but not those who rent. You get no special tax allowances for paying exorbitant rents to exploitative landlords.

Local authority housing is run on a **points system.** To get a choice of housing, you need to accumulate scores of points. You move up the housing list by having more children and living in overcrowded or unhealthy conditions.

It is virtually impossible to get housed if you don't have a child. The points system divides area by status. You need a higher score for some while in others you can get in fairly easily with the minimum of points. Dublin Corporation creates ghettos through its points system: areas that many people refuse. That's how Ballymun, for example, now houses so many single parents. They can never build up a high enough score for other areas, because usually they have only one or two children.

There are about 20,000 people waiting for housing in the Dublin area alone, another 10,000 nationally. Recent government policy has made grants of £5000 available to local authority tenants who opt to buy their own house. The Housing Finance Agency, which provides loans to those on lower income levels, has been inundated with loan applications as a result. Without additional funds this new policy is heading for a bottleneck.

The Homeless

The state in the twenty-six counties takes no legal responsibility for the homeless. After years of inaction, the current government has circulated a bill to change this situation. It is still not part of the law. The Simon Community estimates that there are about 3000 homeless people sleeping rough or in hostels or night shelters, or stuck in county homes and psychiatric institutions because they have no place else to go. This does not include people in temporary accommodation, overcrowding, women without secure accommodation and travelling people.

Homeless people are **criminals** under the vagrancy law, which makes it a crime to beg or 'wander abroad without visible means of support'. Homeless people have difficulty getting social welfare because they have no fixed address. Since 1960, the number of people in psychiatric units has fallen from 26,000 to 13,000. Community care services are poorly funded, and there are very limited detoxification facilities for homeless alcoholics. Homeless people include more and more women and young people. There are 800 homeless young people in the twenty-six counties, cared for by voluntary groups and charities. Only 7% of shelter beds are provided by local authorities or health boards. The proposed government legislation is an attempt to restrict state responsibility by refusing to accept as homeless those who are in this situation 'through their own fault'. Those who have worked with the homeless see this clause as a loophole which will allow local authorities to avoid their responsibilities. After years of negligible funding to Simon, Hope and other agencies concerned with the homeless, it looks as if government legislation **if it comes at all,** will be wholly inadequate.

References

Ad Hoc Womens Group: 'Women in Ireland'. June 1985.

Conradh na Gaeilge: 'Local Broadcasting' submission to Joint Oireachtas Committee on Legislation.

Conradh na Gaeilge: 'A Bill of Rights for the Irish Language'. 1983.

Conradh na Gaeilge: 'Television for the People'. March 1977.

Creative Activity for Everyone: Seminar Report. CAFE 1986.

Department of Social Welfare: 'Statistical Information on Social Welfare Services 1984'. Government Publications Office 1985.

Dublin Lesbian & Gay Men's Collective. Out for Ourselves: The Lives of Irish Lesbians & Gay Men.

Employment Equality Agency: 'Schooling and Sex Roles'. Compiled by Jean Tansey. EEC 1983.

Eileen Evason: On The Edge — A study of poverty and long-term unemployment in Northern Ireland'. Child Poverty Action Group 1985.

Focus Magazine: 'Focus on Youth Employment'. Youth Employment Agency. Issue No. 13 November 1985.

Kieran Hickey: 'The Cinema in Ireland — A Short History' in **The Green on the Screen** programme of Film Festival October 1984.

Irish Times: 'In Search of Sterilisation' by Arminta Wallace. February 7 1986.

Irish Times: 'Emigration — The Hidden Exodus' by Deaglán de Bréadún. February 3/4/5/6 1986.

Irish Times: 'Apartheid on our Doorstep' by Maev-Ann Wren. October 22 1985.

Irish Times: 'Crime — A Tale of Two Cities' by Padraic Yeates. October 23 1985.

Irish Times: 'Far Worse Than In O'Casey's Day' by Frank McDonald. October 21 1985.

Irish Times: 'Drawing New Class Boundaries' by Frank McDonald. October 24 1985.

Irish Times: 'Inner City Renewal — A Vibrant New Era?' by Frank McDonald. March 27 1986.

Irish Times: 'Avoca: A Valley So Sweet?' by Padraic Yeates. March 6 1986.

Irish Times: 'The Burning Issue of Dublin's Dirty Air' by Frank McDonald. April 22 1986.

Irish Times: "Most of old Dublin Needs to be Replaced' by Frank McDonald. April 23 1986.

Irish Times: 'Nuclear Monitoring Poorly Funded' by Frank McDonald. February 17 1986.

Irish Women's Guidebook & Diary: Attic Press.

Magill Magazine: 'Arts for Jobs Sake' by Paddy Woodworth. March 1986.

Magill Magazine: 'The Paper Chase' by Alan Murdock. October 1984.

Magill Magazine: 'Two Weeks in the Life of the Media' by Gene Kerrigan. September 1985.

Magill Magazine: 'The Politics of Drama in R.T.E.' by Paddy Woodworth. March 7 1985.

Magill Magazine: 'The Homeless and the House' by Aileen O'Meara. November 1985.

Magill Magazine: 'The Destruction of Dublin' by Frank McDonald. December 1985.

Magill Magazine: 'Poverty in Ireland' by Fergus Bourke, Bill Doyle and Derek Speirs/IFL Report April 1980.

Frank McDonald: 'The Destruction of Dublin' Gill and Macmillan. December 1985.

Minceir Musli: The Travelling Peoples' Movement. Books of Evidence, I, II and III 1986.

National Campaign for the Homeless: 'Homelessness in the European Community'. January 1986.

Caithriona O'Neill: 'Ownership and Control of the Provincial Press'. Unpublished thesis. NIHE Dulbin 1984.

Raymond Quealty: 'A Description of the Conflicts which have arisen between Current Affairs T.V. and Politicians'. Unpublished thesis. NIHE Dublin 1985.

Radio Telefis Eireann: Annual Report 1984.

Radio Telefis Eireann: Irish National Broadcasting Television and Radio. RTE Information 1986.

Radio Telefis Eireann: The Finances of Broadcasting. RTE Information 1986.

Radio Telefis Eireann: 'Nationwide Community Radio'. R.T.E. 1979.

Report of the Committee for the Rights of Travellers: 1985.

Repeal Section 31 Committee: RTE and the Anglo Irish Agreement. February 1986.

Kevin Rockett: 'Film and Ireland: A Chronicle'. Published by 'A Sense of Ireland' Ltd. March 1980.

Herbert Schiller: 'New Modes of Cultural Domination'. Conradh na Gaeilge. 1978.

Sunday Tribune: 'The Way God Planned It' by Emily O'Reily. Colour Tribune April 20 1986.

Sunday Tribune: 'Lead Pollution Hits City Kids'. February 23 1986.

Contacts

BELFAST

Arts:
Crescent Arts Centre, 2-4 University
Road, Belfast 7.
The Peoples Theatre, Whiterock
Resources Centre, Whiterock Road,
Belfast 12.
Conway Mill, Conway Street, West
Belfast (Conferences/Concerts).

Eating and Drinking:
Carpenter Club, Long Lane, Lr. North
Street, Belfast.
(Women's disco last Friday of month)
Plaza Disco, Lr. Donegall Lane (Friday).
Caper's Restaurant, Great Victoria Street.
Cafe Delbart, Bradbury Place.
Crow's Nest Bar, Skipper Street (off
High Street).
Madden's, Smithfield (Women's night,
Tuesday, upstairs).
Sunflower Club (Women's music,
Summer only).
Red Barn Pub, off Rosemary Street.
The Rotterdam Pub, off Corporation
Street.
Muldoon's Pub, Toombe Street.
Kelly's Cellars, Bank Street.
Le Cafe Hideout, 7 Winetavern Street.
Zero, 2-4 University Road, Belfast 7.

Reading:
Just Books, 7 Winetavern Street, Belfast.
Fortnight Magazine
Shankill Bulletin
Anderstown News
Republican News
Women's News

Centres:
Women's Centre, 18 Donegall Street,
Belfast 12.
Women's Centre, 170A Falls Road,
Belfast 12.
Women's Centre, 195 Whiterock Road,
Belfast 12.

Lesbian/Gay:
Carafriend 222023.

Lesbian Line 222023.
NI Gay Rights Association, 4 University
Street, Belfast 7.

CARLOW/KILKENNY

Kilkenny

Arts:
Kilkenny Design Centre.

Eating and Drinking:
Kytler's Pub, St. Catherine's/Station
Road.

Reading:
Kilkenny Bookshop, St. Kieran's Street.
Book Centre, High Street.

Carlow

Eating and Drinking:
Reidy's Restaurant.
Seven Oaks Hotel.
Health Food Shop, Tullow Street.

Reading:
Carlow Bookshop, Tullow Street.

CORK

Arts:
Triskel Arts Centre, 8 Bridge Street.
Crafts Ireland, Woodford Bourne,
Patrick Street.
The Long Valley, Winthrop Street.
Counihan's, Pembroke Street.
Stripes Rhythm Bar, McCurtain Street/
Bridge Street.
Blues Bar, McCurtain Street.

Centres:
A Woman's Place, Quay Co-op, 24
Sullivan's Quay.

Eating and Drinking:
Harlequin Cafe, Paul's Street.
Quay Co-op Cafe, 24 Sullivan's Quay.
Pizza, Dawn's Square.

Bully's Cafe, Paul's Street.
Halpin's, Cook Street.
The Steeple, Church Street.
Loafers, Douglas Street.
An Crúiscín Lán, Douglas Street.
Jacques Restaurant, Pembroke Street.
Hoagie's, Prince's Street.
The Tea House, Fitzgerald Park,
  Mardyke.

Lesbian/Gay:
IGRM Club, McCurtain Street.
Cork Lesbian Collective, 24 Sullivan's
  Quay, Cork. Tel. 967660.
Cork Gay Collective, 24 Sullivan's Quay,
  Cork. Tel. 967660.
A Woman's Place, Quay Co-op, 24
  Sullivan's Quay, Cork.

Reading:
Mercier Bookshop, Bridge Street.
Egans, Patrick Street.
Lees Books, Lowitt Quay.
Co-op Books, Quay Co-op, 24
Sullivan's Quay.
Liam Russell, Oliver Plunkett Street.

DERRY
Arts:
Orchard Gallery, Orchard Street.
The Strand Cinema.

Eating and Drinking:
The Phoenix Pub, Rosemount.
Carraig Pub, Rock Road/Strand Road.
Andy Coles, Waterloo Street.
Gweedore Bar, Waterloo Street.
Strandid, Strand Road.
Hudson's, Sackville Street.
India House, Carlisle Street.
Taj Mahal, Strand Road.
Acorn Restaurant, Pump Street (day only).
Badger's Place, 18 Orchard Street (pub
  lunch).
Metro Pub, Bank Place (pub lunch).
Igloo Bar, John Street.
Fiorentini's Café, Strand Road.

Reading:
The Bookworm, 16 Bishop Street.
Fortnight Magazine

Centres:
Women's Centre, 7 London Street.
Gordan's Gallery, Ferry Quay Street.
Arts and Craft Centre, Pump Street.
Ship Quay Gallery, Ship Quay Street.
Coleraine Women's Information
  Resource & Craft Centre, 2 Bridge
  Street.

Lesbian/Gay:
Contact: The Bookworm.

DONEGAL
Letterkenny
Arts:
Nothing But McNott, Upper Main Street.

Eating and Drinking:
Pat's Pizza, Market Square.
The Central Bar, Main Street.
The Natural Way Wholefood Shop, Lr.
  Main Street.

Reading:
Community Bookshop (secondhand),
  Main Street.
Browse Awhile Bookshop, Main Street.

DUBLIN CITY
Arts:
Projects Arts Centre, East Essex Street,
  Dublin 2.
Grapevine Arts Centre, 31 North
  Frederick Street, Dublin 1.
Temple Bar Studios, 4-7 Temple Bar,
  Dublin 2.

Eating and Drinking:
Fox and Pheasant, off Capel Street,
  Dublin 1. *Major to Minor*
  (jazz, Wednesdays).
Mulligans, Poolbeg Street.
Doheny & Nesbitt, Baggot Street.
Palace, Fleet Street.
J. J. Smyth's, Aungier Street (Thursday
  and Saturday, women only).
The Coffee Bean, Sth. Leinster Street.
Bewley's, Westmoreland Street, George's
  Street and Grafton Street.

Bananas (vegetarian), Stephen Street,
  Dublin 2.
Pizzeria Italia, Temple Bar, Dublin 2.
  (Tuesday - Saturday).
Charleston Restaurant, Crow Street,
  Dublin 2.
The George (Upstairs), Dame Lane
  (off Sth. George's Street),
  Dublin 2.
Borgia's Restaurant, 6 Lr. Leeson Street,
  Dublin 2.
Focus Point Cafe, 15 Eustace Street,
  Dublin 2.
Shay Beano's Restaurant, Stephen's
  Street, Dublin 2.
The Viking, Dame Street, Dublin 2.

Reading:
Books Upstairs, Market Arcade (off
  George's Street), Dublin 2.
New Books, East Essex Street, Dublin 2.
The Bookshop, Gardiner Place, Dublin 1.
Well Red, Crow Street, Dublin 2.
Sinn Fein, Parnell Square, Dublin 2.
Celtic Bookshop, Harcourt Street,
  Dublin 2.
Fred Hanna, Nassau Street, Dublin 2.
Winding Stairs, 40 Lr. Ormond Quay,
  Dublin 1.
Parsons, Baggot Street, Dublin 4.
Paperback Centre, Suffolk Street,
  Dublin 2.
Easons, O'Connell Street.
Out Magazine
Magill

Centres:
Dublin Resource Centre, Crow Street.
Women's Community Centre, 47-49
  South Richmond Street, Dublin 2.

Lesbian/Gay:
Dublin Lesbian and Gay Collectives, c/o
  Garden Flat, 76 Pembroke Road,
  Dublin 4.
National Gay Federation, Hirschfeld
  Centre, 10 Fownes Street, Dublin 2.
Gay Health Action, Hirschfeld Centre, 10
  Fownes Street, Dublin 2.
Tel-A-Friend (TAF), Gay Information
  and Support Line. Tel. 710608.

Side Two, 26 Dame Lane Dublin 2   (Gay
Disco, Weekends only).
Flikkers, 10 Fownes Street, Dublin 1
  (Friday, Saturday and Sunday).
Sunday - Friday: 8.00 - 10.00 p.m.
Saturday: 3.30 - 6.00 p.m.
Lesbian Line. Tel. 710608 (Thursday 8.00
  - 10.00 p.m.).

GALWAY
Arts:
Galway Arts Centre, Nun's Island.
Druid Theatre, Dominick Street.
Taibhdhearch na Gaillimhe, Sraid Lar.

Eating and Drinking:
The Quay's, Quay Street.
Naughton's, Cross Street.
Nora Crub, Quay Street.
The Bird's Nest, Quay Street.
Mick Taylor's, Dominic Street.

Reading:
Kenny's Bookshop, High Street.
O'Gorman's, Shop Street.
The Pedlar, Quay Street.
Gateway Books, Market Street.

Lesbian/Gay:
Galway Gay Group, P.O. Box 45,
  Eglington Street.

KERRY
Tralee
Arts:
Siamsa Tire Theatre and Arts Centre.

Eating and Drinking:
The Brogue Pub, The Rock.
Val O'Shea, Bridge Street.
Bailey's Corner, Castle Street.
Hennessey's, near St. John's Church.
Railway Bar, Prince Street.
Lynch's, The Spa.
Skillet, The Mall.
Ocean Below, Castle Street.
Stella Restaurant, Castle Street.
Spiral's Bar, Prince's Street.

Reading:
Hurley's Bookshop, Castle Street.
O'Mahony's, Castle Street.

Centre:
Women's Centre, Blackpool, The Spa.

Dingle
Arts:
Leac-a-ré, Strand Street.
Commodum Crafts, Green Street.

Eating and Drinking:
Flaherty's, Strand Street.
The Star Inn, Strand Street.
Carol's Bistro, The Harbour.
The Half Door, John Street.
Daly's, John Street.

Reading:
Café Litreachta, Dykegate Lane.

LIMERICK
Arts:
Belltable Arts Centre, 69 O'Connell Street.

Eating and Drinking:
Piccola Italiano, O'Connell Street.
Peter's Cell, Belltable Arts Centre.
Ted's, O'Connell Street.
Mellick Pub, Glenworth Street.
Whitehouse Pub, O'Connell Street.
Pink Elephant, Bidworth Row.
Mayflower Chinese Restaurant, O'Connell Street.
Tom Collin's Pub, Cecil Street.

Reading:
O'Mahony's Bookshop, O'Connell Street.
Eason's, O'Connell Street.

SLIGO
Arts:
Attic Crafts Co-operative, High Street.
Attic Theatre Co., Castle Street.
Hawks Well Theatre.

Eating and Drinking:
Corkie's Pub, Markievicz Road.

Hennigan's Pub, Wine Street.
McLynn's Pub, Old Market Street.
Comhaltas Ceolteoiri Eireann (Tuesday), Trades Club, High Street.
Hargadon's Pub, O'Connell Street.
Tir na nOg, Wholefood Shop and Cafe, Grattan Street.
Kate's Kitchen, Market Street.
The Venue, Strand Hill.
The Italian Warehouse, Hyde Bridge.
Gulliver's Restaurant, Grattan Street.
Ostie Gillan's, Seafood Restaurant, Rosse's Point.

Reading:
Keohane's, Castle Street.
Broderick's, O'Connell Street.
Tir na nOg Bookshop, Wine Street.

WATERFORD
Arts:
Arts Centre, O'Connell Street.

Eating and Drinking:
Busby's Restaurant, 11 O'Connell Street.
The Chuck Wagon, Broad Street.
Taffy's, Arundel Lane.
Women's Coffee Shop, Arundel Square.
Geoff's Pub, Michael Street.
Jordan's Pub, The Quay.
Downes Pub, Thomas Street.
Suir Inn, Cheekpoint.
Teaser's Restaurant, The Quay.
T. & H. Doolin's Pub, George's Street.
Full of Beans, Shopping Centre, George's Court.

Reading:
Book Centre, Michael Street.
Bevan's, The Quay.
Fitzmaurice, Barronstrand Street.

WEXFORD
Arts:
Wexford Arts Centre, Cornmarket.
Wexford Theatre Co-op, Larkin's Lane, South Main Street.
Spectrum Arts, Silskar Street.

Eating and Drinking:
Thomas Moore Pub, Cornmarket.
Bohemian Girl, North Main Street.
Sean Clarkin, Walker's Mall.
Michael's Restaurant, North Main Street.
The Lotus House, South Main Street.
Natural Food Shop, Lowe Street.
The Cellar Coffee Bar, Wexford Arts
Centre.
Simon's Pub, South Main Street.
Old Granary Restaurant, West Gate.

Reading:
The Book Centre, North Main Street.
Buckland Bookshop, Main Street.
Wexford Bookshop, Walker's Mall.

WICKLOW
Bray
Arts
Bray Community Arts Group, 84 Main
Street, Bray. Tel. (01) 861189.

Eating and Drinking:
The Harbour Bar, The Harbour.
Boomerang Bar, Quinsboro Road.
Tree of Idleness (Greek), Seafront.
O'Shea's Seafood Restaurant, Seafront.
Muffin's Cafe, Main Street.
Molloy's Cafe, Quinsboro Road.

EMERGENCY CONTACTS
Alcoholics Anonymous:
Belfast: 152 Lisburn Road, B9. Tel. (084)
681084.
Cork: Basement Flat, 129 Patrick's Hill.
Tel. (021) 500481.
Dublin: 26 Essex Quay, Dublin 8. Tel.
(01) 774809/714050.
Galway: Ozanam House, St. Augustine
Street. Tel. (091) 67807.
Limerick: Social Services Centre. Tel. (061)
314111.

ALONE:
Tel. (01) 509614.

Ambulance/Fire Brigade:
Tel. 999.

Birth Control:
Belfast: NI FPA, 47 Botanic Avenue, B7.
Tel. (084) 225488.
Well Women's Centre, c/o Open College,
College Square Nth., B2.
Bray (rere Rochalls): Strand Road. Tel. (01)
860401/828088.
Cork: FP Clinic, 4 Tuckey Street, Grand
Parade. Tel. (021) 502906 (appt. only).
Derry: FPA, 18-20 Bishop Street. Tel.
(0504) 260016.
Dublin: FP Centre, 10 Merrion Square,
Dublin 2. Tel. (01) 767852.
FPS, 67 Cathal Brugha Street,
Dublin 1. Tel. (01) 727363
(Adolescent Telephone Service:
ACTS).
IFPA, P.O. Box 908, 15 Mountjoy
Square, Dublin 1. Tel. (01)
744133/729574.
Open Line Counselling, Non-Directive
Pregnancy Counselling, 3 Belvedere
Place, Dublin 1. Tel. 787160.
Well Woman Centre, 73 Lr. Leeson
Street, Dublin 2. Tel. (01)
605517; and 60 Eccles Street,
Dublin 1. Tel. (01) 728051.
Ovulation Method Advisory Service,
16 Nth. Gt. George's Street,
Dublin 1. Tel. (01) 786156.
Dungarvan: FP Clinic, 11 Wolfe Tone
Road. Tel. (058) 42617.
Dun Laoghaire: FPS, 78 Lr. George's
Street. Tel. (01) 850666.
FP, 10 Patrick Street, Dun Laoghaire.
Tel. (01) 803206.
Galway: FP Clinic, 16 Merchant's Road.
Tel. (091) 62992.
Limerick: FP Clinic, 4 Mallow Street. Tel.
(061) 312026.
Navan: IFPA, Trimgate Street. Tel. (046)
21143.
Waterford: 7 Michael Street.

Cherish:
Tel. (01) 682744.

CURA
Tel. (01) 710598.

Drugs Advisory & Treatment Centre:
Tel. (01) 748412.

Epilepsy Association Irish
Tel. (01) 516371/516500.

Legal Aid:
(N.B. It is recommended that you make an appointment)

Belfast: Tel. (084) 235111.

Carlow: St. Catherine's SSC, St. Joseph's Road. Tel. (0503) 31063/31354.

Clare: SSC, O'Connell Street, Ennis. Tel. (065) 28178.

Cork: 24 North Mall. Tel. (021) 500365. Health Centre, O'Brien Street.

Mallow: Tel. (022) 21484.

Donegal: Community Centre, Letterkenny. Tel. (074) 22761.

Dublin: 45 Lr. Gardiner St. Tel. (01) 787295.
 9 Lr. Ormond Quay, Dublin 1. Tel. (01) 741711/748241.
 Aston House, Aston's Place, Dublin 2. Tel. (01) 712177.

Galway: 5 Mary Street. Tel. (091) 61650/62969.

Kerry: St. Patrick's CC, Boherbue, Tralee. Tel. (066) 22351.

Kilkenny: SSC, Waterford Road. Tel. (056) 21685/21409.

Leitrim: Health Centre, Leitrim Road, Carrick-on-Shannon. Tel. (078) 20308.

Limerick: 84 O'Connell Street. Tel. (061) 314599.

Louth: Community Centre, Fair Street, Drogheda. Tel. (041) 32908/36084.

Mayo: County Clinic, Castlebar. Tel. (094) 22333.

Sligo: 11 Teeling Street. Tel. (071) 61647.

Tipperary: CIC, 14 Wellington Street, Clonmel. Tel. (052) 22267.
 SSC, Rossa Street, Thurles. Tel. (0504) 22169.

Waterford: 5 Catherine Street. Tel. (051) 55814.

Westmeath: Dr. Dobb's Memorial Home, Northgate Street, Athlone. Tel. (0902) 72174.

Wexford: Community Services Council, St. Bridget's Centre, Roche's Road. Tel. (053) 23819.

Poisons Information Service:
Tel. (01) 745588.

Rape Crisis Centres:
Belfast: P.O. Box 46, BT27 AR. Tel. (084) 249696.

Clonmel: Tel. (052) 47218.

Cork: P.O. Box 24, Brian Boru Street (post only).
27A McCurtain Street. Tel. (021) 968086.

Donegal: Letterkenny 23067.

Dublin: 2 Lr. Pembroke Street, Dublin 2. Tel. (01) 601470.

Galway: 15A Mary Street. Tel. (091) 64983.

Letterkenny: Tel. (074) 23067 (Monday 10 - 12 a.m.; Saturday 12 - 4 p.m.).

Limerick: 4 Mallow Street. Tel. (061) 41211.

Waterford: P.O. Box 57. Tel. (051) 73362.

Sexual Assault Treatment Centre:
Rotunda Hospital, Dublin 1. Tel. (01) 748111.

Simon Community for the Homeless:
Tel. (01) 711606.

STDs Clinics (Sexually Transmitted Diseases:
Belfast: Royal Victoria Hospital. Tel. (084) 220159.

Cork: Victoria Hospital. Tel. (021) 966844.

Derry: Altnagelvin Hospital. Tel. (080504) 45171.

Dublin: Mater Hospital. Tel. (01) 301937/301122.

Sir Patrick Dun's. Tel. (01) 766942.

Dr. Steeven's Hospital. Tel. (01) 772606/770785.

Galway: STD Clinic. Tel. (091) 64000.

Mullingar: Co. Clinic. Tel. (044) 40221.

Sligo: Sligo Hospital. Tel. (071) 2161.

Waterford: Ardkeen Hospital. Tel. (051) 73321.

Index